Science Under God's Creation

Winsworth Hriinyh

ISBN 978-93-5610-862-2

Published in India 2022 by Pencil

A brand of
One Point Six Technologies Pvt. Ltd.
123, Building J2, Shram Seva Premises,
Wadala Truck Terminal, Wadala (E)
Mumbai 400037, Maharashtra, INDIA
E connect@thepencilapp.com
W www.thepencilapp.com

Author biography

Brought up in a beautiful hilltop, Winsworth Hriinyh was fascinated by nature and often left wondered how the world came into being. From childhood, he loves literature and everything about history. When he finished his high school, he was sent to Engineering College but he intentionally failed the first yearly exam to avoid his Engineering class and eventually left the college and took up Geography for his Bachelor's Degree. When the world was divided into two sections of belief; the belief of the creation of the Universe by Big Bang and the belief of the creation of the Universe in 6 days as affirmed by Creationist, he is ready to show the readers the answer the world wants to know.

CONTENTS

Acknowledgements

First of all, to God, to whom this book is dedicated to. For without Him, nothing is possible.

I acknowledged D. Sholeavi Chahpao for his wonderful suggestion on Technology and God.

I extend my appreciation to Ng. Savini Awardson and K. Ngaoloni Awuh for their supports.

To Pencil Publishing Team for making this book published and helped the world knows more about God.

And not to forget; my mother, brothers and sisters, who stand by me both in good and bad time.

Introduction

Science has become a vital part in our everyday life and in fact, we can never imagine life without science. What science has done, especially in the last two or three centuries is incredible, making human civilization to the greatest extend. The 19th century witnessed one of the greatest periods in the history of science which saw the birth of science as a profession. During this period, the world had witnessed the first steam locomotive in operation, electric motor is built, telephone and light bulb are invented, commercial automobiles are sold and chloroform is used for the first time. Men had even landed on the moon which is one of the greatest milestones in the history of mankind. And science may even help men conquer Mars in the near future.

As the world witnesses the advancement of technologies, men become egoistic, conceited, arrogant, and were not faithful to God anymore, inclining more of their attention towards science than to their God. When science makes life easier and comfortable, men put their trust in the man-made technologies. The discoveries science has made put men into question whether God actually does exist. The more technologies and human civilization advance and progress, the more the existence of God is questioned. If what science has said is true be true. But what is not true shall not muddle men from turning to God.

Chapter 1 Do God Exist

Does God Exist? If God exists, who created Him?
This is one of the most debatable questions between science and religion, especially the Christian for centuries.
Somebody wrote:
"If something comes into being, it must have been prompted by something else. A book has an author. Music has a music artist. All things that begin, that have a start, have a cause to their beginning."
And it is right. If there is nobody to write, a book cannot existed by itself. Or can a house come into existence without being built by somebody? By logical reason, nothing can exist without being created by somebody or something. Everything that existed has a cause to their beginning. No man can claim that he existed on his own, came out of nothing without being born from their mother's womb.
In the same way, Science believes that God doesn't exist for no one had ever created him and he cannot exist by himself. Logically, no one has ever seen anybody creating God and there is no theory and calculation on Earth to prove that God exist. And no one on earth, from the beginning of the creation of the earth to this day has seen God personally. God cannot be seen nor can be touch. One man stated that we have five sense organs i.e, Eye, Ear, Nose, Tongue, and Skin to see, to hear, to smell, to

taste and to feel or touch. Since God cannot be seen, cannot be hear, cannot be smell, cannot be tasted, and cannot be touch. Therefore, God doesn't exist.

No one can deny that no man has ever seen, has ever smelt, tasted or felt God. Does that mean that science was right and the ideology of religions, especially Christianity at fault? Considering the universe, Scientists also once held to the "steady-state" theory that the universe has always existed without beginning, the same way Christian accepted that God existed without beginning. And if God doesn't exist as He cannot be seen, feel or touch; does that make us also think that there is no air, for air also cannot be seen, smell, tasted or touch?

Stephen Hawking, one of the greatest scientists in the 21st century wrote, "I think the universe was spontaneously created out of nothing, according to the laws of science."

He also said, "If you accept, as I do, that the laws of nature are fixed, then it doesn't take long to ask: What role is there for God?"

"Before we understand science, it is natural to believe that God created the universe. But now science offers a more convincing explanation. What I meant by 'we would know the mind of God' is, we would know everything that God would know, if there were a God, which there isn't. I'm an atheist." Hawking made this controversial statement in 2014 during an interview with Pablo Jauregui, a journalist from El Mundo, a Spanish language newspaper. In his final book 'Brief Answers to Big Questions' published by Bantam Books, he made several statements on God. He wrote, "If you like, you can say the laws are the work of God, but that is more a definition of God than a proof of his existence"

"We have finally found something that doesn't have a cause, because there was no time for a cause to exist in. For me this means that there is no possibility of a creator, because there is no time for a creator to have existed in."

When asked what happened before the Big Bang, he answered, "There was no time before the Big Bang."

According to Stephen Hawking, there is no place for God in theories on the creation of the Universe. He said, "There is no God. No one created universe and no one directs our fate." In his book, 'The Grand Design' he stated that the Big Bang was an inevitable consequence of the law of physics and the belief in a creator was not incompatible with science."

He went on to say in his final book that events before the Big Bang are simply not defined, because there's no way one could measure what happened at them. And since events before the Big Bang have no observational consequences, he said that one may as well cut them out of the theory, and say that time began at the Big Bang.

He boldly said in his final book, "We have this one life to appreciate the grand design of the universe, and for that I am extremely grateful. My prediction is that we will know the mind of God by the end of this century."

Albert Einstein who was considered one of the greatest scientists in the world also wrote the following words in German-language letter to philosopher Eric Gutkind on 3rd January 1954, "The word 'God' is for me nothing but the expression and product of human weaknesses, the Bible a collection of venerable but still rather primitive legends. No interpretation, matter how subtle, can (for me) change anything about this. For me the Jewish religion like all other religions is an incarnation of the most childish superstition."

Most of the scientists believed that the universe cannot be created in just six days. They established the principle of the creation of the universe on Big Bang theory. And the history of our universe dated our universe was 13.7 billion years old that begins with a massive expansion that blew space up like a gigantic balloon which is still expanding and claimed that the evidence supporting the idea is extensive and convincing. They also claimed to have discovered a predicted thermal imprint of the Big Bang and there is no object older than 13.7 billion years.

"All of these things put the Big Bang on an extremely solid foundation. The Big Bang is an enormously successful theory." said astrophysicist Alex Filippenko of the University of California, Berkeley.

When a student asked James D. Watson, who was also known as the 'father of DNA' if he believes in any gods, answered, "Oh, no. Absolutely not. The biggest advantage to believing in God is you don't have to understand anything, no physics, no biology. I wanted to understand."

Many books have been published worldwide testifying (with their philosophy) the non-existence of God with the like of 'The Non-Existence of God' by Nicholas Everitt, 'The God Delusion' by Richard Dawkins, 'Western Atheism: A Short History' by James A. Thrower, 'Atheists: The Origin of the Species' by Nick Spencer, 'Atheism: A very Short Introduction' by Julian Baggini, 'Atheism: The Case Against God' by George H. Smith, 'God is not Great' by Christopher Hitchens, 'Arguing for Atheism' by Robin Le Poedevin, 'Atheism: A philosophical Justification' by Michael Lou Martin, 'Everybody is Wrong about God' by James A. Lindsay, 'God wants you to be an Atheist: The

Startling Conclusion from a Rational Analysis' by Gary J. Whittenberger, 'Atheism Explained: From Folly to Philosophy' by David Ramsay Steele. (There are still many books on Atheism which are not listed here). Not only atheist but even once a devout Christian happens to reject the teaching of Christianity, one of those is John W. Loftus who was once an ordained minister of the Church of Christ with three degrees in Christian's Faith to his name became an atheist and had authored ten books denouncing the Christian's faith and the existence of God. In one of his book 'Unapologetic: Why Philosophy of Religion Must End' published in 2016, he said, "There really are no sacred scriptures. They do not exist. No deity inspired anything because no deity exists. All so-called revealed religions are false."

He also said in his blog referring to the time of WWI where more than 20 million of people had died and 20 million more injured, "God is good, right? Bullshit. His only excuse is that he doesn't exist."

In the book, 'God: The Failed Hypothesis' written by Victor J. Stenger, said in the first chapter, that the evidence made by theologians and theistic scientists about the existence of God is not sufficiently convincing the majority of scientists and overwhelming majority of prominent American scientists has concluded that God does not exist. "If God exists, where is he?" He questioned.

He also referring on the compilation essay 'The Impossibility of God' by Michael Martin and Ricki Monnier to justify the non-existence of God in which it stated that All-Virtuous Being cannot exist because a being can be properly said to be virtuous if it can suffer pain or be destroyed.

Let us see what they said in their definitional disproofs: (please refer to the original essay for details if you must)

AN ALL-VIRTUOUS BEING CANNOT EXIST

God is (by definition) a being than which no greater being can be thought.
Greatness includes greatness of virtue.
Therefore, God is a being than which no being could be more virtuous.
But virtue involves overcoming pains and danger.
Indeed, a being can only be properly said to be virtuous if it can suffer pain or be destroyed.
A God that can suffer pain or is destructible is not one than which no greater being can be thought.
For you can think of a greater being, one that is non-suffering and indestructible.
Therefore, God does not exist.

WORSHIP AND MORAL AGENCY

If any being is God, he must be a fitting object of worship.
No being could possibly be a fitting object of worship, since worship requires the abandonment of one's role as an autonomous moral agent.
Therefore, there cannot be any being who is God.

THE PROBLEM OF EVIL

If God exists, then the attributes of God are consistent with the existence of evil.
The attributes of God are not consistent with the existence

of evil.
Therefore, God does not and cannot exist.

A PERFECT CREATOR CANNOT EXIST

If God exists, then he is perfect.
If God exists, then he is the creator of the universe.
If a being is perfect, then whatever he creates must be perfect.
But the universe is not perfect.
Therefore, it is impossible for a perfect being to be the creator of the universe.
Hence, it is impossible for God to exist.

A TRANSCENDENT BEING CANNOT BE OMNIPRESENT

If God exists, then he is transcendent (e.i., outside space and time).
If God exists, he is omnipresent.
To be transcendent, a being cannot exist anywhere in space.
To be omnipresent, a being must exist everywhere in space.
Hence it is impossible for a transcendent being to be omnipresent.
Therefore, it is impossible for God to exist.

A PERSONAL BEING CANNOT BE NONPHYSICAL

If God exists, then he is nonphysical.
If God exists, then he is a person (or a personal being).
A person (or personal being) needs to be physical.
Hence, it is impossible for God to exist.

THE PARADOX OF OMNIPOTENCE

Either God can create a stone that he cannot lift, or he cannot create a stone that he cannot lift.
If God can create a stone he cannot lift, then he is not omnipotent.
If God cannot create a stone that he cannot lift, then he is not omnipotent.
Hence, God is not omnipotent.

How many of you understand their statement? Have you now realize what they said is right and doubted about God?
The above mentioned equations mean to flouted the existence of God is emotive. We must first understand that everything exists in the universe co-exists. There is plant that needs animal (and human being) to survive and animal also needs plant to live. From life science or biology, we are been taught that plant and animal depends on each other for respiration in which plant gave oxygen to animal and they get carbon-dioxide from animal. Just as we have coexistence, we also have divergence. We call one thing good when we have bad thing. When there is something beautiful, we have something that is ugly too. If two things look exactly the same, we cannot call one thing beautiful and the other one unpleasant. If virtue exist, something that is vice will co-exist with virtue because without vice, we cannot call anything virtue. Since we know that vice exist, virtue also exist. Therefore, there can exist a virtue without been destructible as vice exists. God is indestructible and nothing can make Him suffer on purpose because no being is greater or superior than Him but He can be sad or unhappy when His people turn away

from Him.

"Do I have any pleasure at all that the wicked should die? Says the Lord God, and not that he should turn from his ways and live?" - Ezekiel 18: 23 (NKJV)

Here, the scripture tells us that God find no pleasure when people go against him and die unrepentant. Let us also look at Genesis 6:6 which says, "And the Lord was sorry that He had made man on the earth, and He was grieved in His heart."

When the people He had created don't walk in the path of righteousness, He also feels sad. At this point, atheist questioned why God would create man if He already knew that He would one day regret creating man if He is omniscient. Does that mean He is not all-knowing God? Does that mean God does not exist? This is where God gave the greatest gift of all to man. A freewill. He gave us freewill to make our own choice. The decision we made can destroy or build anything around us. God's greatest gift on the thing He had ever created is the knowledge and understanding that He had instilled unto man apart from any other living organism and the freewill to make our own choice and decision. In fact, God can make all of us go according to His plan, to be obedient without any gripe, and living under His incantation. But would that makes Him happier? He chose to allow us to make our own choice. Without freewill, who will glorify and appreciate for the thing He had created and will God contented with no one to appreciate his creation? It is your choice whether to appreciate Him or denouncing Him. God made you to enjoy his creation and appreciate it but He also did not forbid you to speak against Him if you choose to, because you have your own freewill, however, the decision you made is what will make you happy or regret later. Therefore, God who is All-Virtuous can exist, and He really exists.

Worship is an act of showing reverence to somebody or something that is superior to the worshiper. To worship doesn't mean that the worshiper must completely submit to that he was worshipping against his own freewill. Unfortunately, there are many people on earth who worshipped that is not of God. The world has worshipper of cow, the sun, the moon, the stars, ancient place or object, an idol make of wood, iron, silver or gold, or image of their so-called deity. If we shall not worship God who is the source of all things, who is there more befitted for worship?

We know that evil exist, then goodness does co-exist with it because if there is no goodness, nothing can be call as evil. Evil is connected to Satan just is goodness and righteousness is associated with God. Therefore, if evil exist, Satan does exist, and if Satan exist, then God does exist. Just look at our lives; nobody can claimed to not see wickedness and evil such as stealing, lying, killing, gossiping, hatred, adultery, murder, fighting, betrayal or quarrelling. Those are all the works of evil. However, we have goodness in our society as well. This proves that there is evil as well as righteousness exist which mean that both God and Satan exist.

"Then God saw everything that He had made, and indeed it was very good….."

– Genesis 1:31 (NKJV)

At the time of creation, everything was good. He set the sun and the moon in its place, the sun to rule during the day and the moon during the night. He made every kind of animals, some to be food, some to help and other to be man's companion. He also made all kind of birds and fishes and every green grasses and plants so that they will co-exist with each other. Then finally, God gave the gift of freewill to man.

"And the Lord God commanded the man, saying, Of every tree of the garden you may freely eat; But of the tree of the knowledge of good and evil, you shall not eat, for in the day that you eat of it you shall surely die." - Genesis 2: 16 - 17 (NKJV)

Here, God commanded man not to eat the fruit, also warned the consequence of eating the fruit but He also allowed man to make his own choice. If God did not give the freewill to man, He won't have to create that tree of the knowledge of good and evil that man should fall in it. If God chose man to completely obedient to Him, He will not made that tree of the knowledge of good and evil because man will completely obedient to Him no matter what, even without the knowledge of good and bad. God knows the mind of man but He allows man to have their own freewill. Since evil exist from the very beginning, man falls into its trap and disobey God. When man (Adam) disobeyed God, imperfectness entered the world.

Oxford dictionary defined 'transcendent' as 'beyond or above the range of normal or physical human experience, or, surpassing the ordinary, or, exceptional'. Cambridge dictionary defined the same to even lower phrases, such as, 'greater; better; more important; or, going past or above all other'. So, based on its definition, 'transcendent' simply mean 'incomparable or better or greater than all things. Its explanation has nothing to do with anything 'limitation'. Therefore, transcendent being can exist anywhere because there is no certain limit set on it. Since God is spirit, He can exist anywhere without any exertion.

God is not like us who has an intransferable physical body. He has no definite shape. God is spirit which is nonphysical but can also be a personal being if He wants to because He can do anything and everything. If God cannot transform into a physical being, then He is not God. Therefore, He can be both nonphysical and personal being. Hence, it is possible for God to exist and God does exits.

One of the most exciting parts of the equation is 'God is not omnipotent' if He cannot create what He cannot lift or if He cannot lift what He has created. This evaluation is purely based on human weakness which shows our vocabulary 'omnipotent' wrong. Nobody will invent thing which doesn't have any purpose. Some invention may go wrong but the intention of the inventor is to create something that can be useful. Likewise, God doesn't need to create anything without purpose. In the human context, something that God cannot lift should be too huge for space to hold. And what is the purpose of creating that huge object which is not useful at all? We know that our universe which science hasn't measure its expanse yet, is hanging on nothing. So, God doesn't need to lift things like universe that is hanging (because what He will create anything bigger than the universe will also hang on nothing) and God doesn't need to create anything which is bigger than the space itself.

Great personalities in the field of science like Elie

Mitchnikoff, Lubos Motl, John Forbes Nash Jr. Alfred Nobel, Mark Oliphant, Linus Pauling, John Allen Paulos, Ruby Payne Scott, Wilhelm Reich, Charles Frances Richter, Richard J. Roberts, Ethan Siegel, Nikolai Vavilov, James D. Watson, Steve Wozniak, George Beadle, Hans Bethe, Robert Cailliau, Sean M. Carroll, James Chadwick, Frances Crick, George Washington Crile, Irene Joliot-Curie, who were discoverers and inventors amenably express their disbelief on the existence of God. Having seen many great personalities in the list of atheist, many people will be tempted to belief in their views. But there are also many great personalities who believed in God. The names of such man and women who are familiar to even high schooling students are Blaise Pascal, Isaac Newton, Andre Marie Ampere, Nicolaus Copernicus, Galileo Galilei, Michael Faraday, Charles Babbage, Guglielmo Marconi, Alessandro Volta, and Mary Anning.

Science may have discovered what they claimed the cause of the creation of the universe; matter colliding each others to form this huge mass, basing on the Big Bang theory. But scientists don't know what preceded the Big Bang and what created those matters. So the very beginning of the universe still remains in dark for science. As science progress rapidly, its followers became too conceited in their own thinking, making themselves equivalent with God or even greater than him, for when claiming to have God not existed, they're trying to made themselves a god that people should adore them. But there's one thing we all should know that science was created or discovered by man not long ago. And worshipping it makes people a slave of their own creation.

According to science, there is no theory on Earth to prove the existence of God but there is also no theory on Earth to prove the non-existence of God. I can boldly maintain the non-believer on the existence of God as a feeble person at heart. For if we have faith, there is no point arguing about something which is beyond our understanding.

If we questioned the existence of God because He cannot be seen or touch, we also cannot say air does exist because the air we breathed cannot be seen or touch either. As scientist claimed that God cannot existed by his own, let's say for now that there is no God who created the universe. That suggested that the universe is created on the contrary to what Christian believes, by something else. And science is trying to prove 'that something' is the Big Bang. I think this is where science had failed. Instead of proving their work understandable to the people, it throwed themselves into quizzical situation with more thing to elucidate.

What is big bang?

We know that as they asserted that nothing can exist by its own, how can big bang which cannot created itself came into being? Logically, there should be something which created the Big Bang. That proves that there should be something exists before the Big Bang. What is that 'something' that created the Big Bang? It is beyond their understanding and have no idea what come before the Big Bang. If science put question on who created God, then the same question can be raise on big bang and matter. What created the big bang or the matter? And what is that, that created the matter?

Who created God?

The most direct answer is the one supplied by the Scriptures (Holy Bible) themselves. From it, we know that no one created God and He did not come from anywhere. He has no beginning and will have no end. That says, He is the eternal and self-existing being.

God is eternal

In the book of Isaiah 40: 28 (NKJV) says, “Have you not known? Have you not heard? The everlasting God, the LORD, The Creator of the ends of the earth, neither faints nor is weary. His understanding is unsearchable.”

And the book of Romans (16:26) and 1 Timothy (1:17) supplemented the same scripture.

“But now made manifest, and by the prophetic Scriptures made known to all nations, according to the commandment of the everlasting God, for obedience to the faith.”

“Now to the King eternal, immortal, invisible, to God who alone is wise, be honor and glory forever and ever. Amen...”

And Psalmist exalted God with the following words “Before the mountains were brought forth, Or ever You had formed the earth and the world, Even from everlasting to everlasting, You are God.”

Before anything came into being, God was there. Before Big Bang was formed, God was there. He created everything. He even created the Big Bang as science called, that one day; man should study the universe from it. And when science discovers what precede the Big Bang, God will be there.

And the book of Exodus (3:14) revealed God as Self-existing Being through Moses. “And God said to Moses, ‘I AM THAT I AM’: and He said, ‘Thus shalt thou say unto

the children of Israel, I AM has sent me to you."
"And He said to me, It is done! I am the Alpha and Omega, the Beginning and the End….."

Revelation 21: 6 (NKJV)

"I am the Alpha and Omega, the Beginning and the End, the First and the Last."

Revelation 22: 13 (NKJV)

All these scriptures clarified that God is the beginning and no other being has ever exist before Him. And He will be the end that no other being will last longer than Him. The phrases thus indicated that no one has created God because He was the first that has ever exists and nothing has ever existed before Him. Therefore, God has self-exist before no other thing exists.

If we still cannot accept the existence of God in the biblical view, let us take a look at logical views.

First, it is understandable that the universe must have been created by something because things exist and science also proved that the universe was not a self-existed object which is created by something. Before the universe was formed, there should be something that existed before to create the universe. And scientist claimed it; Matter. They based the creation of the universe on Big Bang theory. What is Big Bang theory anyway? The question is; what created the matter and what is that matter that created matter?

Since we all know that something does now exist, one must logically conclude that something has existed always because if there was a time nothing at all existed, then there would be absolutely nothing today. If there is nothing but nothing, there can never be something out of nothing. Scientific calculation also proved that ZERO (nothing) plus ZERO (nothing) equals ZERO (nothing). Therefore, there was something that exists to develop into something else just as evolution takes place every billion or million years in the context of science. Since we all know that matter now exist, science cannot claim that there was a time when nothing does exist or their mathematical calculation, erroneous.

If nothing cannot produce something, and yet something exists, then it is mathematically proven that something has existed to produce something. As we can see now that thing exists, there is something existed eternally. The question is; what is the "something" that has been in existence always? And this 'something' could be of material in nature or non-material. We can see that material things are those that can be touch and can be seen while non-material the opposite and that everything we see in this universe is made up of materials. And the 'something' could also be non-material which could be a 'spirit'.

The book of gospel John (4:24) testify that God is a spirit. "God is a Spirit: and those who worship Him must worship him in spirit and truth."

As there is possibility that non-material thing could exist before material in nature exist, there is every possibility that God exist before anything in the universe came into being. Since God is all-powerful and all-knowing, He can created things without any intricacy. God is beyond our imagination, and who are we to question about the existence of God?

Chapter 2 Do God Has a Wife

Many historians and researchers claimed to have finally found out that God did have a wife, 'Asherah'. They also claimed that the ancient Israelites worshipped both God and Asherah. The prominent among them is a British theologian and broadcaster, Francesca Stravrakopoulou, now a senior lecturer in the department of Theology and Religion at the University of Exeter.

She wrote; "After years of research specializing in the history and religion of Israel, however, I have come to a colorful and what could seem, to some, uncomfortable conclusion that God had a wife."

J. Edward Wright, president of both the Arizona Center for Judaic Studies and Albright Institute for Archaeological Research also claimed that many English translations prefer to translate 'Asherah' as 'Sacred Tree'. He wrote; "This seems to be in part driven by a modern desire, clearly inspired by the Biblical narratives, to hide Asherah behind a veil once again."

Their researches were mainly based on the ancient texts; inscription on pottery, amulets and figurines. It can be true that the inscription of pottery described the name of the goddess; for it is true that the Israelites indeed worship Asherah. Sadly, it is clearly mentioned many times in the Old Testament about the worshipping of the goddess Asherah alongside their God. However, the worship of the

goddess only raises the anger of the Lord, their God. If Asherah was the wife of God, He won't mind his people worship her as well. In the context of men, who won't love to see his own wife honored by the people?
No one live long enough to see the beginning of the earth. And no one is godly enough to live with God in heavenly abode to witness what God do every day. Now, what they claimed about God's personal life is unreasonable. God did inspire no one to keep his record on pottery or figurine with the exception of the Holy Bible.
Let us look at some of the contexts in the Holy Bible which mentioned about the goddess Asherah.
In Judges 3: 7 (NIV), it reads, "The Israelites did evil in the eyes of the Lord; they forgot the Lord their God and served the Baals and the Asherahs." By worshiping Baal and Asherah, the Israelite sinned instead of pleasing God.
"And the Lord will strike Israel, so that it will be like a reed swaying in the water. He will uproot Israel from this good land that he gave to their forefathers and scatter them beyond the river, because they provoked the Lord to anger by making Asherah poles." -1 Kings 14: 15 (NIV)
"They also set up for themselves high places, sacred stones and Asherah poles on every high hill and under every spreading tree." - 1 Kings 14: 23 (NIV)
"Ahab also made an Asherah pole and did more to provoke the Lord, the God of Israel, to anger than did all the kings of Israel before him." - 1 Kings 16: 33 (NIV)
"Now summon the people from all over Israel to meet me on mount Carmel. And bring the four hundred and fifty prophets of Baal and the four hundred prophets of Asherah, who eat at Jezebel's table." - 1

Kings 18:19 (NIV)

"They set up sacred stones and Asherah poles on every high hill and under every spreading tree." - 2 Kings 17:10 (NIV)

"They forsook all the commands of the Lord their God and made for themselves two idols cast in the shape of calves, and an Asherah pole. They bowed down to all the starry hosts, and they worshiped Baal." - 2 Kings 17:16 (NIV)

"He rebuilt the high places his father Hezekiah had destroyed; he also erected altars to Baal and made an Asherah pole, as Ahab king of Israel had done. He bowed down to all the starry hosts and worshipped them." - 2 Kings 21: 3 (NIV)

"He took the carved Asherah pole he had made and put it in the temple, of which the Lord had said to David and to his son Solomon, "In this temple and in Jerusalem, which I have chosen out of all the tribes of Israel, I will put my Name forever." - 2 Kings 21:7 (NIV)

"They abandoned the temple of the Lord, the God of their fathers, and worshiped Asherah poles and idols. Because of their guilt, God's anger came upon Judah and Jerusalem." - 2 Chronicles, 24: 18 (NIV)

"Even their children remember their altars and Asherah poles beside the spreading trees and on the high hills." - Jeremiah 17: 2 (NIV)

All these scriptures written in the Holy Bible show us that the Israelites indeed worshipped Asherah. As she was worshipped by the people as goddess, it is not impossible to have her name engraved on stone or on pottery. And finding the remains is not surprising. Christian cannot deny the Israelites worshipping the goddess. With the finding of inscription on the potter and on other relic, the atheist now taken a further step by claiming that Asherah is the consort of God, and Christian/Bible scribes omitted out later from the Bible with monotheistic agenda. However, the good news is, they cannot do much harm to Christian religion with their theories. To elucidate the allegation of God having a wife, there is something we need to reason with.

First: Nowhere in the Holy Bible did the word 'wife of God' appeared, and the people who claimed or proposed this, is just trying to defame the holiness of the Holy Bible and God with their conspiracy theories.

Second: It (Asherah) was nowhere being recommended for worship, but rather condemned anyone who worship it.

Third: Asherah is just a wooden idol chiseled out by skilled craftsman, then decorated with silver and gold to make it look more beautiful. It is not really a goddess but a piece of wood.

We cannot term or confer the name 'consort of God' to Asherah merely because she is been worshipped by the Israelites alongside their God. We also cannot confer to her 'consort of God' merely for being a female 'deity' as people used the term.

On the contrary, the Holy Bible clearly stated that Asherah is merely a piece of man-made wooden idol who cannot move nor speak nor think or eat or drink. This is what God said to the Israelites through prophet Jeremiah about the so-called foreign gods/idol(s).

Jeremiah 10: 3-5 (NIV): "For the customs of these peoples are worthless; they cut tree out of the forest, and a craftsman shapes it with his chisel. They adorn it with silver and gold; they fasten it with hammer and nails so it will not totter. Like a scarecrow in a melon patch, their idols cannot speak; they must be carried because they cannot walk. Do not fear them; they can do no harm, nor can they do any good."

Let's have a look at some verses in the Holy Bible about Asherah.

Exodus 34:13 (NIV): "Break down their altars, smash their sacred stones and cut down their Asherah poles."

Deuteronomy 7:5 (NIV): "This is what you are to do to them: Break down their altars, smash their sacred stones, cut down their Asherah poles and burn their idols in the fire."

Deuteronomy 12:3(NIV): "Break down their altars, smash their sacred stones and burn their Asherah poles in the fire; cut down the idols of their gods and wipe out their names from those places."

Deuteronomy, 16: 21(NIV): "Do not set up any wooden Asherah pole beside the altar you build to the Lord your God."

Judges 3:7(NIV): "The Israelites did evil in the eyes of the Lord; they forgot the Lord their God and served the Baals and the Asherahs."

Judges 6: 25(NIV): "That same night the Lord said to him, "Take the second bull from your father's herd, the one seven years old. Tear down your father's altar to Baal and cut down the Asherah pole beside it."

1 Kings16: 33 (NIV): "Ahab also made an Asherah pole and did more to provoke the Lord, the God of Israel, to anger than did all the kings of Israel before him."

2 Kings17:16(NIV): "They forsook all the commands of the Lord their God and made for themselves two idols cast in the shape of calves, and an Asherah pole. They bowed

down to all the starry hosts, and they worshiped Baal."
2 Chronicles 19: 3(NIV): "There is, however, some good in you, for you have rid the land of the Asherah poles and have set your heart on seeking God."
2Chronicles 24: 18(NIV): "They abandoned the temple of the Lord, the God of their fathers, and worshiped Asherah poles and idols. Because of their guilt, God's anger came upon Judah and Jerusalem."

All these scriptures clarified that God is not happy with the worship of Asherah pole. Instead, He ordered the kings and his people to destroy it to prevent them from sinning against Him. Worshipping it is condemnable. How many times did God allowed the enemies of Israel to defeat them for worshipping other gods? The Israelites were so arrogant and conceited that they, many times fall into worshipping of other gods forgetting the Lord their God and many times God let their enemies ruled over them.

We now knew that there is nothing supernatural in her. And God condemned Israel for worshipping it. Many still believed goddess Asherah to be a 'goddess of fertility'. If that's true, well and good; for we could pray to her for fertility. But since she is just a piece of wood, what can she do? What good can a piece of wood do for us?

Now, if Asherah was the consort of God, why would he order his people to tear down the Asherah pole? Asherah is not at all a goddess.

Atheist raises another similar question.

"If Jesus Christ is really the son of God; God must have a wife. Who is the mother of Jesus Christ apart from Virgin Mary?"

Atheist presumed that Jesus must have a mother in

heavenly abode just as he has a mother on earth. This presumption is purely based on earthly thing or theory. God, being the supernatural being, we cannot compared him with the earthly theory. It is true that every human born child came through a woman after been impregnate by a man. However, the birth of Jesus Christ is of different thing. He was also called the Son of Man because He too came into this world through a human mother, but we must remember that He was not the seed of a human father. He was conceived by the Holy Spirit. His birth was foretold, and what name he should bear is also been made known to his parents (human parents) before his birth.

The question is, if He exists before his incarnation to the earth, God must have a wife who give birth to Jesus Christ or God's his father must have created him like Adam.

Jesus Christ was not the son of God by birth from the human flesh or by birth of heavenly being nor was created. Jesus did not become the son of God for fulfilling the prophecy of the scripture. He was with God before the creation of the earth and he was the same as God. In gospel John, we have learned that through Him God made all things. It is the same as God made all things because of him. For God did not made anything without Him (Jesus).

Chapter 3 Creation of the Universe

Formation of the Sun

Secular Scientist thinks that the sun was formed about 4.6 billion years ago, from a giant rotating cloud of gas and dust known as solar nebula. As the nebula collapsed because of its gravity, it spun faster and flattened into a disk and its mass is about 109 times the diameter of the Earth. They said that most of the material was pulled toward the center to form the sun. Scientist, according to their theory, claimed that the sun and its atmosphere are divided into several zones and layers. The solar interior is made up of the core, radiative zone and the convective zone and the temperature in the core is about 15 million degrees Celsius which is driven by nuclear reactions. Above the core is consists of the photosphere, chromosphere, a transition region and the corona and beyond that is the solar wind, an outflow of gas from the corona. Scientist believes that the visible part of the sun is about 5,500 degrees Celsius hot and has enough nuclear fuel to stay much as it is now for another 5 billion years.

Formation of the Universe

According to science, the universe was formed by big bang. The first person to proposed that the universe began with an explosion was Belgian scientist George Lemaitre. Then in 1929, astronomer Edwin Hubble discovered that the universe is expanding. One second after the big bang, it is said that the universe was filled with neutrons, protons, electrons, anti-electrons, photons and neutrinos. About 380,000 years after the big bang, matter cooled down and the universe began to emerge from the cosmic dark ages 400 million years after the big bang, in which first stars and galaxies were formed from a clumps of gas and the expansion of the universe slowed down. Then, according to their theory, dark energy began the speeding up the expansion of the universe again. But what give rise to the big bang? NASA admitted that it is beyond the model of the big bang, which Stephen Hawking also said that time before the big bang cannot be analyze and should therefore just say that time begin from the big bang. Interestingly, it is said that the universe is made up of atoms which constituted about 4.6 percent of the universe while 72 percent is made up of dark energy and the remaining percent is formed by dark matter.

Creation of the Earth

The perception of how the Earth was created is an interesting one. And science trying to elucidate the formation of the Earth is alluring. The question of how the Earth was created is a hot topic debating for years between science and religion, especially Christianity. Science claimed to have based their theory on mathematical and logical reason while religion, especially Christianity based their views on faith and the word of God, the Holy Bible. Now let us first look into how science has explained about the formation of the Earth.

One source affirmed the Earth is thought to have been formed about 4.6 billion years ago by collisions in the giant disc-shaped cloud of material that also formed the sun. It is also claimed that many scientists think the sun and the rest of the solar system formed from a giant rotating cloud of gas and dust known as the solar nebula. As the nebula collapsed because of its gravity, it spun faster and flattened into a disk. Most of the material was then pulled toward the center to form the sun. After the sun is formed, planets and their moon are thought to have formed from the solar nebula, the disc-shaped cloud of gas and dust left over from the sun's formation. The same is with the formation of the Earth. But as the Earth is different from other planet, we will focus more on how the Earth was created or formed.

According to science, the Earth was formed along with other planets by collisions in the giant disc-shaped cloud of material. Volcanic outgassing probably created the primordial atmosphere and then the ocean, but the early atmosphere contained almost no oxygen. Much of the earth was molten because of frequent collisions with other bodies which led to extreme volcanism. While the Earth was in its earliest stage, a giant impact collision with a planet-sized body named Theia is thought to have formed the moon. Over time, the Earth cooled, causing the formation of a solid crust, and allowing liquid water on the surface.

Science tried to explain the formation of the Earth in three ways. The first and most widely accepted theory is the Core Accretion Model, the second theory is the Disk Instability Model and the third, the Pebble Assertion.

The Core Accretion Model

In the Core Accretion Model, the solar system was a cloud of dust and gas known as a Solar Nebula. As it spins, gravity collapsed the material, forming the sun in the center of the nebula. And with the rise of the sun, the remaining material began to clump up, drawing small particles together, bound by the force of gravity, into larger particles. The solar wind swept away lighter elements, such as hydrogen and helium, from the closer regions, leaving only heavy, rocky materials to create smaller terrestrial object like Earth. But farther away, the solar winds had less impact on lighter elements, allowing them to combine into gas giants. In this way, asteroids, comets, planets, and moons were created.

The Earth's rocky core formed first, with heavy elements colliding and binding together, while the lighter material created the crust, in which the planet's magnetic field was probably formed around this time. Then gravity captured some of the gases that made up the planet's early atmosphere.

Collisions from icy bodies such as comets and asteroids likely deposited much of the Earth's water on its surface and because the Earth is in the Goldilocks zone, the region where liquid water neither freezes nor evaporates but can remain as a liquid, the water remained at the surface, which many scientists think plays a key role in the development of life.

The Disk Instability Model

According to this model, gas giants needed to evolve rapidly to seize significant mass of lighter gases although the core accretion model works fine for terrestrial planets. The process takes several million years and at the same time, the core accretion model faces an exodus of young planets as it is likely to twirl into the sun in a short amount of time. Then clumps of dust and gas are bound together early in the life of the solar system and eventually, these clumps slowly compact into a giant planet. These planets can form faster than the core accretion, allowing them to trap the rapidly vanishing lighter gases and quickly reach an orbit-stabilizing mass that keeps them from death-marching into the sun.

Pebble Accretion

This model suggested that the disk would have cleared itself out in about 1 million to 10 million years as its gas evaporated and its dust spiraled into the gravitational pull of the Sun. The big planet such as Jupiter and Saturn somehow packed together a core about 10 earth masses before the disk vanished.

The biggest planets in the solar system may have gotten their start from the smallest of rocks, about pebble sized that formed 4.5 billion years ago from dust and ice swirling around the young sun. Research strengthened support for the idea that these primordial pebbles rapidly melded into the core of gas giants such as Jupiter and Saturn.

The idea of Pebble Accretion was put forth in 2012 by Michiel Lambrechts and Anders Johansen of Lund University in Sweden. It was said that this idea able to explain how a planetary core could form rapidly, as friction with gas in disk would have slowed pebbles enough for them to be accreted onto an embryonic planet.

The biggest challenge to core accretion is time — building massive gas giants fast enough to grab the lighter components of their atmosphere. Recent research shows how smaller, pebble-sized objects fused together to build giant planets up to 1000 times faster than earlier studies.

"This is the first model that we know about that you start out with a pretty simple structure for the solar nebula from which planets form, and end up with the giant-planet system that we see," study lead author Harold Levison, an astronomer at the Southwest Research Institute (SwRI) in Colorado, told Space.com in 2015.

"They showed that the leftover pebbles from this formation process, which previously were thought to be unimportant, could actually be a huge solution to the planet-forming problem." Levison said.

At the formation of the earth, science claimed that there was no water and the atmosphere contained almost no oxygen. They believed that meteorites and comets could have supplied the water. And as the Earth cooled down, clouds were formed and produced water in the form of rain. Ocean was then created by the rain in about 4.4 billion years ago.

The abundant of oxygen came only 1.8 billion years after the creation of the Earth if the concept of science is to believe. The Big Bang theory stated that the atmosphere of the Earth at its formation hold almost no oxygen. Oxygen was then emerged in abundant when bacteria began to produce oxygen in 2.8 billion years ago. But it was toxic at that time and much life on Earth may have died or extinct due to the rising of oxygen level.

The history of Earth enlightens us about the development of the Earth from its formation to the present day. And as science continues to study Solar System, most of the branches of natural science also described the past of the earth by studying geological change and biological evolution. They will tell us more about how our Earth and other planets were formed and how our Earth has changed from the creation to this present day.

Stephen Hawking, one of the greatest scientists in the world in the 21st century, in his final book 'Brief Answer to Big Questions' says, "I think the universe was spontaneously created out of nothing, according to the law of science. If you accept, as I do, that the laws of nature are fixed, then it doesn't take long to ask. What role is there for God?"

He also said, "Did God create the quantum laws that allowed the Big Bang to occur? I have no desire to offend anyone of faith, but I think science has a more compelling explanation than a divine creator."

Hawking further wrote, "We have finally found something that doesn't have a cause, because there was no time for a cause to exist in. For me, this means that there is no possibility of a creator, because there is no time for a creator to have existed in." And he declared that there was no time before the Big Bang.

Now that science did its best to explain about the formation of the Earth, I wonder how many of you believe in their theory about the creation of the Earth.

Although, they had proved that there are other eight planets apart from our Earth in the solar system, and discovered each and every moon of the planets and also the stars in the universe, how they form remains a subject of debate because the exact theory of their creation haven't been made as science still continue to study about the universe. Tomorrow, they will come up with a better concept about the universe.

As per their claim, God has nothing to do with the creation of the Earth; deviated at the conjecture of creating this massively weight Earth in a single day by an individual. In their view, God cannot and doesn't exist because there is no being who exist before Him to create God for God himself cannot be existed out of nothing.

The question of 'Who created God?' is a question which

even left many Christian mystified. And taking advantage of such Christian individual, science tried to distract those minds to their so-called theory. But one day, they will come up with a conclusion that God is behind every creation. And the waiting for such submission won't be long.

I am here, as a believer of God, to argue with science about the creation of the Earth. I'm here to prove that their theory about the creation of the Earth and the development of the Earth is not what they think it was. As per their claim, oxygen, which is essential for all living organism emerged only after 1.8 billion years after the formation of the Earth, as stated earlier, was produce by bacteria which is a living organism. They maintained that the first life on Earth occurred in 3.8 billion years ago where carbon dioxide composed the main element in the Earth's atmosphere at that time which is 1 billion years before oxygen was found in abundance. If oxygen is produced by bacteria, what is the component which created bacteria? And how many bacteria were needed to produce oxygen which is now constituted of about 20.95% of the total air in the atmosphere? And how carbon-dioxide which maintain as the main element in the atmosphere 3.8 billion years ago constitute of only 0.04% in the atmosphere now? Life science taught us that we human being as well as the animal breathe in oxygen and breathe out carbon-dioxide. Therefore, logically, we release carbon-dioxide every time we breathe out. As the population of people increases every year and plants and trees diminishes, where could those carbon-dioxides gone? If their theory is based on logical reason, it can be said that oxygen should be weaken and carbon-dioxide elevated as the population of human being and animal who consumed oxygen to survive and discharge carbon-dioxide increases while the plants that releases oxygen were shrinking due to deforestation and expansion of human civilization. But what is the proportion of their contents in the atmosphere? We are taught that living organism need oxygen for survival, but if oxygen is first produced by bacteria, who is needed whom?

According to science, water was first produced by meteorites and comets. If that is true, how water is shaped needed an explanation because meteorite and comet is not solely water body but more likely of planet or rock type. And generating water body which covers more than 70% of the Earth's surface by them is not likely to take place. They also established their theory on the earth cooling down to formed clouds which in turn created water in the form of rain and ocean was then created by rain which is taken placed 200 million years after the formation of the earth. This hypothesis is also not likely to take place logically.

According to science, the Earth was formed along with other planets by collisions in the giant disc-shaped cloud of material. It is agreeable that the Earth was formed out of giant disc-shaped cloud of material. But what is the thing that formed the material which formed the earth and other planets?

Scientists claimed that Earth was not created by God because God does not exist and was not possible because there is no time for God to have existed in. The same question is with science. If there was no time before the Big Bang, how is it possible that Big Bang came in existence? How can big bang explode if there was nothing at all? If there is absolutely nothing before the Big Bang, there will still be nothing, for there cannot be something come up out of nothing. To create or form the universe that holds the sun, eight planets and their moons, meteorites, comets, asteroids, dwarf planets and millions of stars, most of them bigger than our planet Earth, would require a gigantic force and materials and now science tries to make us believe that all these things were formed by the Big Bang. How from out of nothing, becomes this colossal universe suddenly?

Science began the history of the universe at the Big Bang. What happen before it? They were clueless too. Stephen Hawking, whom many people regarded as one of the greatest scientists in the modern world, was theoretical physicist and cosmologist, but could not find what lies before the Big Bang. He said, "Since events before the Big Bang have no observational consequences, one may as well cut them out of the theory, and say that time began at the Big Bang. Events before the Big Bang, are simply not defined, because there's no way one could measure what happened at them." I'm sure he had tries to find out what lies before the big bang but why did he fail? Science study only what can be seen and touch. If we cannot find the answer, should we just leave it like that? Scientist boasted that their theories are based on logical reason, but if they cannot prove what precede the big bang, where is their logical reasoning?

Pre events of the Big Bang remain a mystery to science until now though science has developed so much. But if their theory is settled to define about the creation of the universe, a clearer explanation should be given to support their reason. Since there's no formula to compute on it and no equipment to measure it, it is useless that we try reasoning what is not yet discovered. Big Bang should be the end of the question now until science made further discovery on it because we know science is still ever changing and progressing with something new coming up time to time.

Let us look at what the Christian's Holy Bible says about the creation of the universe. The Holy Bible, many assumed that it was purely written by human being and take it for granted. It was indeed written by the hand of man and is not handed down to us as a completely written book by God Himself. But every single word in the Holy Bible was written by man inspired by the spirit of God. That is why it was said, "I testify to everyone who hears the words of the prophecy of this book: If anyone adds to these things, God will add to him the plagues described in this book. And if anyone takes away from the words of the book of this prophecy, God shall take away his part from the Book of Life, from the holy city, and from the things which are written in this book….." - Revelation 22: 18 & 19 (NKJV)

And in Deuteronomy 4:2 (NKJV) also read, "You shall not add to the word which I command you, nor take from it, that you may keep the commandments of the Lord your God which I command you."

"Heaven and earth will pass away, but My words will by no means pass away…." Luke 21:33 (NKJV)

Genesis, the first book of the Holy Bible and in first chapter, we can find the story of the creation of the earth and of the universe.

In the beginning God created the heavens and the earth. Now the earth was formless and empty, darkness was over the surface of the deep, and the Spirit of God was hovering over the waters. And God said, "Let there be light," and there was light.

In verses 9 and 10 (KNJV), we found, "And God said, "Let the water under the heavens be gathered together into one place, and let dry land appear." And it was so. And God called the dry land Earth, and the gathering together of the waters He called Seas. And God saw that it was good."

The earth wasn't created or formed out of materials from Big Bang and water is not produced by meteorites or comets. Just as science affirmed that the earth was formless in the beginning, the Holy Bible also maintained that the earth was without form and was covered with darkness when God first created it. Therefore, God created light, separated the sky from the earth, water and dry ground were gathered separately. Then God created all kind of plants.

The following verse read, "Then God said, 'Let the earth bring forth grass, the herb that yields seed, and the fruit tree that yields fruit according to its kind, whose seed is in itself, on the earth' and it was so."

God also created all kind of fishes that lives in the sea, birds that fly in the sky and animals that crawl and move in the land.

Then God said, "Let the waters abound with an abundance of living creatures, and let birds fly above the earth across the face of the firmament of the heavens." So God created great sea creatures and every living thing that moves, with which the waters abounded, according to their kind, and every winged bird according to its kind. And God saw that it was very good. Then God said, "Let the earth bring forth the living creature according to its kind: cattle and creeping thing and beast of the earth, each according to its kind." And it was so. And God made the beast of the earth according to its kind, cattle according to its kind, and everything that creeps on the earth according to its kind. And God saw that it was good. V: 20, 21, 24 and 25.

Finally, God created mankind. Not just created them in the likeness of fishes, birds or animals, but in His own image.

Then God said, "Let Us make man in Our image, according to Our likeness, let them have dominion over the fish of the sea, over the birds of the air, and over the cattle, over all the earth and over every creeping thing that creeps on the earth." So God created man in His own image; in the image of God He created him; male and female He created them. V: 26 and 27.

Planets and its moon and stars were there before human race begins but it is not long since man discovered them. We can see millions of them up in the sky but we never knew what they are, how big they are, how bright and how heavy they hold until astronomers discovered them.

With the help of science, men were able to find out what is there in the universe. They were able to detect which is the nearest to Earth among them. The brightest star has been discovered as well. Before the coming of science, it is believed that the sun revolves round our Earth however, science proved it wrong.

As science advanced from generation to generation, the discovery of even the farthest stars were made possible. Thanks to Galileo Galilei who discovered the greatest number of discoveries. He was the first person tell the world in 1610 A.D. that the evening star we see with our naked eyes is actually a planet, like ours, Venus. Then

Mercury was first discovered in 1939 by Zupus. Mars, the red planet as we called was discovered by Christian Huygens in 1659.

Galileo Galilei discovered Jupiter, the biggest planet in the universe in 1610. He also shows the world that Jupiter had four moons orbiting the planet. That same year, he discovered Saturn as well.

Uranus was discovered on March 13, 1781 by William Herschel. The credit of the discovery of Neptune goes to the three men, namely; Urbain Le Verrier, Johann Gottfried Galle, John Couch Adams. They discovered Neptune on September 23, 1856.

Pluto was once considered to be the smallest and nine planet in the universe orbiting the sun until its status was questioned following the discovery of objects in the Kuiper belt in which Pluto located and thus the International Astronomical Union reclassified Pluto as a dwarf planet was discovered by Clyde Tombaugh on February 18, 1930 from Lowell Observatory.

Astronomers have discovered many other stars. We were told that they had measured the distance from earth, mass, mean density, surface temperature, surface area of each planet and thousands of stars by means of scientific calculation. Their discoveries were indeed amazing and their works should be extolled. However, they cannot claim they had the knowledge of each star in the universe for it is too gigantic for a mere human being to understand of it. Nevertheless, we can assure that they will discover many more about the universe in the coming time. From this, we understand that men do not have infinite knowledge of everything that are here on earth or in the universe. For if men have the knowledge of everything, then the claiming of 'There is no God' can be true. But, as God is omniscient, He knows that men will be conceited, therefore, no matter how wise a person can be, He did not put the knowledge of everything to a man. But He will let men to find out bit by bit about the universe so that men will continue their effort of finding out everything in the universe and that men should stayed marveled at what He had done.

Rotation of the Earth: Nature or By God?

From the school, the subject of science taught us that the earth does rotated on its axis and also revolves round the sun without stopping for a single second. Even a junior student knows that our earth rotated once every 24 hours. Not only our planet Earth does rotate but all the other planets in the universe; except that their speed of rotation and direction of rotation varied. Some rotate at slower pace and some rotates quicker than the other. We were been told that the planet Venus, the second planet closest to the sun rotates once taking 243 Earth days which mean we will have to wait 243 days long for the sun to raise again if it set today if we happen to live there. Likewise, the planet Mercury also rotated at slower pace than our planet which takes 59 of our Earth days to rotate once. Just imagine how awkward it will be if our Earth also rotate at that slow pace like Venus, a woman conceive today would give birth just after a day at Venus. Why our planet Earth takes just 24 hours to rotate once has a purpose.

Our planet Earth rotating once in just 24 hours makes the world friendly to life. It makes us easier to adapt our life as there is no extreme of both; day or night, hot or cold. If our earth rotated at much slower pace than now, we would have seen lesser day or night in our entire life, for a day will take longer to get dark and when it is dark, it will also take longer time to dawn. And it is for sure that no one of us wants the day to be much longer than today or the night too long. A longer period of daytime would mean we will have a longer period of working hour which would make us required to use more energy to meet the assignment given to us.

And our body will stop functioning normally if we continuously exhausted our body, resulted to effecting our daily performance, fatigue, insomnia, diminished appetite, changing mood that leads to anger, anxiety or confusion, or weakening our immune system. And a longer period of nighttime would make our sleeping hour longer and most of us won't like that either. These day and night period is just right for us; not too long and not too short.

And what will happen if our Earth rotated too fast? Day and night will become shorter and it will become very hard to adjust our timetable. We would have to get up in the morning before we get enough sleep and getting inadequate sleep everyday would resulting our body function abnormally. And since our working hour will have to be shorter than now, we have to either work faster or harder to meet the people's demand or if we stick our work limit as it is today, it will be unproductive. One bad thing is that, we will have to face natural calamity like hurricane, cyclone or tsunami more often and more dreadful and destructive because the hurricane or cyclone will spin faster. Earthquake will be stronger and more destructive. Those living in the coastal area would witness more of tsunami because the tide of the ocean or the sea would harsher and many islands and landmasses of the earth will emerge under the water and consequently, people around the world will face dearth of land to dwell in.

If our Earth didn't spin at all, there will be no day and night. We will have 6 months long night and 6 months long day in a year. That mean, we will have only one day and one night in a year. Those experiencing day will always have hot day and those experiencing night will always have cold night. And the surface temperature will depend on where you are. You will face the wrath of the sun always if you're living in the equatorial line facing the sun or you will experience cold forever if you're living in another part of the world opposite to the sun or in the southern or northern hemisphere. And the magnetic field of the Earth will no longer exist and hence the gravitational force of the Earth will also change which would make life on the planet inhabitable.

But how and what makes our Earth able to rotate on its axis and also revolves round the sun? Science told us that our Earth is able to rotate on its axis due to magnetic field of the Earth and is slightly slowing down as there is a little bit of friction between the tides which is cause by the gravity of the moon and turning of the earth. We were also told that there was a vast cloud of dust and gas in our solar system in the beginning and when those clouds began to collapse; it formed a giant disk that rotate faster and faster around the sun, thus formed the Sun at the center of the universe. Clumps of matter of all sizes is said to have collided often when the planets were forming which knock off pieces and sending each other into spinning and the gravity of bigger objects captured those smaller one in orbit, thus those smaller objects become their moon. Likewise, scientist also thinks that our moon is created when an object about the size of Mars collided with our Earth which knocked out a chunk of material which becomes the moon setting our Earth spin at faster rate. And they estimated that a day in the early formation of our Earth was just about 6 hours long.

We knew that an object must be pushed by a force in order to keep it moving. Let's say, a spinning top will stop eventually when the force and energy is completely consumed. In order to keeps the spinning top moving a force is required. But some scientists and devotee of science said that this concept is utterly wrong. In their point of view, an object in motion tend to stay in motion and an object at rest tend to stay at rest and thus a force is required to make it stop and not to keep it moving. They explained that, since the Earth is rotating on its axis, there is no force working to counter the rotation that it don't need to have any input energy to keep it spinning except that the tidal effect of the moon makes it slowing down.

They (scientists) explicated that as the Earth was formed out of a nebula that collapsed, and when it collapsed, it began to rotate. And as stated earlier, clumps of matter that collided with each other often knocks off pieces and sending each other into spinning. As the Solar System spun more rapidly, it flattened out into a disk with a bulge in the middle. The Sun formed from the bulge at the center of this disk, and the planets formed further out and they inherited their rotation from the overall movement of the Solar System itself. All the materials in the Solar System gathered together into planets, asteroids, moons and comets over the course of some hundred million years and then the powerful radiation and solar winds from the young Sun cleared out everything that was left over. Thus, without any unbalanced forces acting on them, the inertia of the Sun and the planets have kept them spinning for billions of years and will continue to spin as long as they collide with an object in the futures. So what started the earth and the planets and their moon and even the sun rotates in the first place? By logical reason, there should be a kind of force which pulled those materials toward the point which form the sun. Because if there is no force at all, all the materials will be in station and we may need to know what lies in the force or what created that force. And why do almost all the planets and even the sun spin in the same direction? They said that the reason behind the spinning in the same direction is because they all formed together in the same Solar Nebula, billions of years ago. But I said again, what force makes them spinning?

I don't know how many of you agreed with the explanation made by science and its devotee, scientist. What they discovered about the rotation of the Earth and other planets, the comets and meteors, the stars and the Moon and even the Sun (the Sun doesn't orbit any planet in the universe but it does spin on its axis once taking 27 days) is one of the greatest achievements in the history of human civilization. Before Copernicus discover that our Earth revolve around the sun in 1514, though the belief of the earth revolves around the sun was first proposed by Aristarchus of Samos as early as 3rd BC, people in the olden days thought that our earth was stationary and the sun revolves around the Earth. Even Aristotle and Ptolemy believed that our earth is the center of the universe, surrounded by the sun, the moon, the stars and other planets. With the help of science, we were able to get the knowledge of law of planetary motion, that it is the sun which is stationary, and the planets revolves around it. We still might believe in the theory of Aristotle that the Earth stood still and is in the center of the universe if science didn't exist.

But there are things which need more explanation on their part. Before the materials in the universe collided each other forming the powerful radiation and solar winds from the Sun clearing the leftover of the material which now allow all the planet revolving around the Sun on its orbit without losing its course and collide each other again, what force makes them collided with each other? And which object collide which object? They didn't say anything. As we know from their description on the Solar System, all the planets with the exception of Venus and Uranus, rotates in anti-clockwise, and so do the Sun. If one object hitting the other, it is possible that they go spinning in opposite direction or orbiting the Sun in opposite direction. But all their theories demonstrated that only Venus and Uranus spin in clockwise among the planets and all of them orbiting the Sun in the same direction. They said that the reason behind the spinning in the same direction is because they all formed together in the same Solar Nebula. Their theory on the formation of the universe and of the Earth maintained that it is thought to have been formed about 4.6 billion years ago by collisions in the giant disc-shaped cloud of material that also formed the sun. Gravity slowly gathered this gas and dust together into clumps that became asteroids and small early planets called planetesimals. Then these objects collided repeatedly and gradually got bigger, building up the planets in the Solar System, including the Earth. The collision of the element of gas and dust and binding them together formed

all the planets and their moons and other objects which are left out from the formation of the Sun. It is acceptable that the planets orbit around the Sun due to the Sun's gravity force. But what is the force that made the objects collide each other in the first place? The Sun doesn't exist as it is but was formed just like the planets and the moon except that the Sun was formed a bit earlier, therefore, there should be a force before that to allow the element to collide each other to create the Sun. So, what is that force?
They (scientist) explicated that an object in motion tend to stay in motion and an object at rest tend to stay at rest and thus a force is required to make it stop and not to keep it moving. If that is true, what force makes the object into motion in the first place? If there is no force at all, there will be emptiness and no object will be able to move if there is no force act on it. It is quite not clear how the Sun and the Universe were formed if there is no force act upon them.
As we can see that Jupiter, the biggest planet with radius of 69,911km and also the fastest spinning planet in the Solar System taking just 10 hours to rotate once its axis and travels around the Sun at a speed of 13.07 km/s or 29,236 miles per hour with a mass of 1.8982x1027Kg which is 2.5 more massive than all the other planets in the Solar System and so heavy that it would take 318 times Earth's masses to equal Jupiter's mass colliding a smaller object like Mars having its mass measure up to 6.4171x 1023kg which is equal to just 0.107 of Earth's mass or Pluto with mass of 1.31x1022kg or 0.00218 of earth mass or as tiny as the biggest Asteroids, Ceres which is about 583 miles across its circumference or Comet Hale-Bopp, one of the biggest comet which is 60 Km in radius won't make much

significant of its motion. Instead, it is possible to make the other object into spinning or travel faster. But the farther away the planet or an object is from the Sun, the slower it travels. Let's take for example:

Mercury, the fastest planet in the universe which travelled at a speed of 47.87 km per second or 107,082km/h taking just 88 Earth days to orbit around the sun is the closest to the Sun. Our Earth travels at a safe speed of 29.78 km/s or 66,615 miles per hour is at third planet from the Sun. And the dwarf planet, Pluto makes one orbit around the sun at a speed of 10,623 miles per hour. Taking that, according to their concept, the planets in the Solar System orbit around the sun in the same direction as the Sun rotated with its movement and its gravity acting as the source of force. It is said the planet Mercury is only 57.91 million km or minimum 28.5 million miles or maximum at 43.5 million miles because it does not orbit in perfect circle away from the Sun whereas the planet Neptune is 4.495 billion km or 2.795 billion miles away from the Sun. Will the effect and the gravity of the sun still works on it which is more than 4 billion kilometer away? It is said that the strength of the Sun's magnetic field is only about twice as strong as the Earth's field. Pluto is still farther away from the Sun than Neptune and it is amazing that Pluto orbit around the Sun.

The largest planet in the Universe, Jupiter with gravity of 24.79 m/s2 has 79 known moons and 53 of them were officially named such as Europa, Ganymede, Lo, Callisto, Megaclite etc. The second planet with the highest number of moon is Saturn which has 62 confirmed moons of out which 9 of them were still awaiting an officially named. It has gravitational force of 10.44 m/s2. Then Uranus with

8.87 m/s2 gravity has 27 moons and Neptune can boast of having 14 moons. We all know that our Earth has one moon, Luna. Even the dwarf planet, Pluto (discovered in 1930 and was then downgraded to Dwarf Planet from the title of Planet in Aug 24 2006 by the International Astronomical Union (IAU) as it did not meet the criterion of the planet) with a gravity of just 0.62 m/s2 has four moons such as Charon, Hydra, Nix Styx and Kerberos.

Ganymede, 1.428 m/s2, the largest moon of Jupiter and Titan, the largest moon of Saturn with gravity of 1.352m/s2 has higher gravitational force than Pluto. If Pluto having just 0.62 m/s2 gravity has four moons orbiting around it, why shouldn't Ganymede or Titan have moon? Even Triton with 0.779m/s2, the largest moon of Neptune has a greater gravitational force than Pluto. Then why was Pluto have not just one but four moons while Triton doesn't have any object orbiting around it?

They asserted that the reason why the planet Venus whose gravity of 8.87 m/s2 having no natural satellite or moon is because Venus is too close to the Sun that its moon once believed to have exist was taken away by the Sun due to its strong gravitational force. If this theory is to be accepted, why is Neptune which farther away from the Sun and having greater gravitational force than Saturn and Uranus has fewer moons than them?

Scientific calculation on distance and mass is based on assumption and not factual. For there's no string long enough to measure even the distance between the moon and the earth or measuring the circumference of the Jupiter or any other planet. No one has gone to Mars and measure its surface.

In his article 'Problem with the Assumptions' Andrew A. Snelling, himself a geologist, explained how the scientific method for dating rocks failed. According to him, to date a radioactive rock, geologists have to first measure the 'sand glass' in the top glass bowl (the parent radioisotope, such as uranium-238 or potassium-40). Then they measure the sand grains in the bottom bowl (the daughter isotope, such as lead-206 or aragn-40 respectively). Based on these observations and the known rate of radioactive decay, they estimate the time it has taken for the daughter isotope to accumulate in the rock. In his Assumption 1, he said that no geologists were present when most rocks formed, so they cannot test whether the original rocks already contained daughter isotopes alongside their parent radioisotopes. In assumptions 2, Snelling explained that unlike the hourglass, the radioactive 'clock' in rocks is open to contamination by gain or loss of parent or daughter isotopes because of water flowing in the ground from rainfall and from the molten rocks beneath volcanoes. Hence, it can mix and contaminate it. Because of such contamination, the less than 50-year-old lava flows at Mt. Ngauruhoe in New Zealand yield a rubidium-strontium 'age' of 133 million years, a samarium-neodymium 'age' of 179 million years, and a uranium-lead 'age' of 3.908 billion years. Then in assumption 3, he said that physicists have carefully measured the radioactive decay rates of parent radioisotopes in laboratories over the last 100 or so years and have found them to be essentially constant, and that they have not been able to significantly change these decay rates by heat, pressure, or electrical and magnetic fields, so, geologists have assumed these radioactive decay rates have been constant for billions of years. (for further information, please refer to original article, https://answeringenesis.org/geology/radiometric-dating/radiometric-dating-problems-with-the-assumptions/)

Like he said, we cannot take for granted whatever science told us. By faith, we believed in the 6-days creation; God with His infinite wisdom created the universe in 6-days' time. And by assumption, scientist believes that the universe is more than 4 billion years old. Sadly, most people in the world and even many Christian believe the earth might indeed billions of years old because science said so, seeing the advancement of science in technology.

Despite all their effort to prove their supremacy in every aspect, science will always fall short when it comes to God. Their discovery about the Universe or Solar System amazed us. For a commoner, the ability to discovered or see a far-off object in the sky calculated to more than 3 billion kilometers away from us like Pluto or Saturn is a wonder, hard to believe. But science makes it possible. Yet, their theory becomes a question when we look into it carefully, just like they are not ready to accept what the Holy Bible said. And the above account tells us that science cannot prove what God has hidden from us (human being) despite their highly advanced technology and understanding.

The best answer we can find is in the Holy Bible. In Genesis chapter one, we can find the story of the creation of the Earth and of the Universe by God Himself. Since God is omniscient, He knows what is best when He created anything. He knows that a day too long or a night too long will not be good for living; that is why He made day and night in the most favorable time to adjust, not too long and not too short. Having a day and night by reason is not possible without making the Earth or the Sun turn or rotate; and since He knows that if He made the Sun orbit around the Earth to make day and night, it would travel too fast which would cause disaster in the Universe, that is why He made the Earth rotated on its axis. God knows living organism cannot survive if the Earth's temperature is too hot or too cold; that is why He placed our Earth in the best place in the Universe, not too close to the Sun and not too far from the Sun. He made the Moon orbit around our Earth in order to keep the night more favorable for men. And in His wisdom, He didn't created moon to have its own light to shine because if it has, it would cause catastrophe on the Earth and its inhabitant when the light of the Sun and of the Moon shine together at the same time; that is why, He allows the moon to shine from the reflection of the Sunlight and made the Moon orbit around the Earth in such a manner that it would only shine during the night most of the time. And He keeps the Earth rotating and revolving around the Sun at moderate speed to allow the Earth's condition favorable for inhabitance.

Jesus said, in the book of Matthew, that the sun will grow dark, the moon will no longer shine and the stars will fall from heaven, and the powers in space will be driven from their course when His disciple asked about His coming. If Jesus had not known that the universe has a formality of its own, He would not have said so. Since He was there when the universe was created, He knows how the universe works and also know that at the command of God, the creator, everything in the universe will cease working as well.

Chapter 4 Evolution of Life

It has been claimed that life according to science, appeared on earth about 4.1 billion years ago, after some million years of earth formation, with more than 99 percent of all species that ever lived on earth until today are estimated to be extinct. As to how rock and water are formed, is explained that the earth cooled after the formation of the earth is completed and thus its surface was solidified to a crust which it was also explained briefly in the previous chapter.

Another source affirmed the Earth to be over 4.5 billion years old, with its oldest materials, a zircon crystals, being 4.3 billion years old. Interestingly, Science also claimed a single-celled micro-organisms known as prokaryotes to be the first living organism on Earth. As per their assertion, they have preserved the oldest rocks on the planet from where the earliest evidence for life on earth is been able to extracted. They made another claim to have found another oldest life on earth on rocks in Greenland which hold the fossils of 3.7 billion years old colonies of cyanobacteria.

Still, another source declared the history of life on Earth began about 3.8 billion years ago, with single-celled prokaryotes as the first living thing on earth. A source asserted that multi-cellular life evolved much later and it's only in the last 570 million years that the kind of life forms we are familiar with began to evolve, starting with arthropods, followed by fish 530 million years ago. Then came the land plants in about 475 million years ago, and lastly, mammals which appeared on earth some 200 million years ago. Whether to believe or not, our species, Homo sapiens, arrived the last on earth, dating 200 thousand years ago.

Let us look at the geological time period, divided into eighteen periods and epochs, with each period and epoch separated by a major geological or paleontological event according to science.

1. Archean era

Archean era which began from about 3.8 billion years ago and ended in 2.5 billion years ago, was said that it was during the Archean era that life first arose on Earth, where there were no continents but just a small island in a shallow ocean with carbon dioxide composed the main element in the atmosphere.

2. Cryogenian period

The Cryogenian period begins about 850 million years and ended 215 million years later. Life during the Cryogenian consisted of tiny organisms - the microscopic ancestors of fungi, plants, animals and kelps all evolved during this time.

3. Ediacaran period

The period begins in 625 million years ago and ended in 545 million years ago, and all life in this period was soft-bodied where there were no bones, shells, teeth or other hard parts. As soft bodies don't fossilize very well, remains from this period are rare, it claimed.

4. Cambrian period

The Cambrian period which begins in 545 million years ago and lasted for about 50 million years, is famed for its explosion of abundant and diverse life forms where life had diversified into many forms and many ways of living: animals now swam, crawled, burrowed, hunted, defended themselves and hid away.

5. Ordovician period

Animals and plants were begun to explore the margins of the land during this period which begins in 495 million years ago. The Ordovician period is said to be ended with a mass extinction in about 433 million years ago.

6. Silurian period

The Silurian period created a new type of ecosystem for marine life, with bony fish made their first appearance and plants became more established on land. This period ended in about 417 million years ago.

7. Devonian period

The Devonian period which began in 417 million years ago is also known as the Age of Fishes, since several major fish lineages evolved at this time as the temperature became more suitable for the living things. The period ended 63 million years later.

8. Carboniferous period

Reptiles first appeared in this period as oxygen levels on earth increases considerably. The Carboniferous period which lasted for about 64 million years ended 290 million years ago.

9. Permian period

The Permian started with an ice age (290 million years ago) and ended with the most devastating mass extinction the Earth has ever experienced (248 million years ago).

10. Triassic period

As the environmental conditions become more favourable, it opened up some evolutionary opportunities, resulting to the evolution of the very first mammals and dinosaurs. Triassic period began 248 million years ago and ended in 205 million years ago.

11. Jurassic period

The first birds and some of the dinosaurs appeared during this period. Jurassic period began after the mass extinction of the Triassic period ended in 142 million years ago.

12. Cretaceous period

This period witness the extinction of dinosaurs and North and South America were drew apart from Europe and Africa, also the Indian Ocean was formed at this time. Cretaceous period ended in 65 million years ago.

12. Palaeocene epoch

The period which began about 65 million years ago make many new creatures such as mammals and birds evolved as a result of the extinction of dinosaurs and other big reptiles. It ended in 5.8 million years ago.

13. Eocene epoch

Forests thrive and trees grew even in polar regions during this period, with Himalayas and Alps were also founded. The Eocene epoch lasted just 11.1 million years.

14. Oligocene epoch

Many fast-running prey and predator species appeared. This epoch began in 33.7 million years ago and ended in 23.8 million years ago.

15. Miocene epoch

The apes appeared and by the end of this epoch, the ancestors of humans split away from the ancestors of the chimpanzees to follow their own evolutionary path. Miocene epoch began in 23.8 million years ago and ended in about 5.3 million years ago.

16. Pliocene epoch

Ice at the North Pole became permanent and grassland and tundra thrived during this epoch. The Pliocene epoch lasted just 1.7 million years, compared to lengthy period at the beginning of geological time period.

17. Pleistocene epoch

Our species evolved during this epoch. It began in 2.6 million years ago and ended in 11.7 thousand years ago.

18. Holocene epoch

The Holocene is the current geological epoch which started some 11,500 years ago. And human being appeared in this epoch.

In order to determine the age of the fossils, they (scientists) used Relative Dating and Radiometric Dating using the remnant of fossil found on the rock surface, however, how reliable could it be to determine the actual age of objects as old as million-years-old? It will be hard to prove because fluids may have penetrated cracks in the stone, allowing newer microbes in to older rocks. It is no impossible the decay of the older microbes to lose intact in the rocks after many years.

Which is the first living organism on earth is still a question. According to one source, Prokaryote (a single-celled organism without membrane-bound nuclei or cell organelles) is the oldest living organism in the world. A 3.7 billion-year-old colonies of cyanobacteria, found in a rocks in Greenland is another contender of the first living organism in the world. The earth is about 4.54 billion years old and some suggested that life began as early as 4.5 billion years ago. If we are seeking the fact, we need an undisputed evidence and not suggestion. If we have to search for the oldest living organism in the world, we should go for the source that suggested life begins in about

4.5 billion years ago. But what is that organism who is 4.5 billion years old? So, the world is once a bacteria world (a single-celled organism) with no other living organism found beside it. Then the world becomes a multi-cellular life form followed by invertebrate organism world and lastly, a vertebrate organism world. And the youngest of all living organism is human being, whom man are being transformed or evolved from an ape. So, the direct descendant of human being is an ape.

It is an interesting story of how human being is being evolves from an ape, another type of monkey still living in the world. But, how true is the story? Are we really descended from an ape? I would rather not call an ape, my ancestor for I am completely different from an ape that still found today. I walked differently from an ape. I think differently from an ape. My habit is quite different from an ape. It is not really nice but I cannot climb tree like an ape. But, I'm proud to say that I can run much faster than an ape. I'm wondering why science still trying hard to prove that we are the descendent of an ape, an animal that is not really us?

Secular scientist believes and persuaded the people to believe that man has no special place in the universe which means that we came into this world by cosmic accidents like any other being on the planet- evolution. And their assumption would mean that we will also evolve into something else one day when the right time of the universe came. If what they preaches is true, there is no meaning of life. There is nothing worth living a pure life or suffered in the name of righteousness. And Charles Darwin is right to say about the surviving of the fittest in his famous book 'Origin of Species' if we are not descended from Adam.

But since we are the descendent of Adam, we are a special creation, a completely different creature from any other living organism.

If their theories are to believe, an ape should not be given the sole credit as the ancestor of human being, for before the arrival of the ape, there are other living creatures from which ape also descended from. When we look back at the aforementioned history of life on earth based on life science, question can be arises as to how multi-cellular life evolved from a single-cellular organism. And how vertebrate living creature evolved from invertebrate living creature is a question needed an explanation. Human being or any other vertebrate living creature constitutes of different organs like; bone, muscle, blood, nerve, fluid, whereas a single-cellular organism should constitutes of only one cell, and they cannot be move for it do not have leg, cannot see for it do not have eyes, or cannot be fed for it do not have mouth or stomach because they were constitute of only one cell. If their cell is an eye, their whole body will be an eye and if their cell be call muscle or leg or stomach, their whole body will be only single cell of muscle or leg or stomach. And how long does it live?

Imagine the earth where there is no plant, water and no living thing on earth at the formation of the earth. It is understandable that the Earth will be like Mars or any other planet where no living organism found on them even after billions of year of their formation. As no living organism evolved in the beginning, there still no living organism found in them. It is true that our Earth is different from other planet, being the only planet where essential substance for living is found, there is one thing that should be understand; why only Earth and no other planet?

In order to survive, living organism needs air and water. Yet, in the beginning of the formation of the Earth, water is not included in the particles which formed the Earth. One source stated that as the Earth cooled, cloud is formed and thus created rain and oceans were created by rain. Another source mentioned comets and meteorites from the outer asteroid could have been contributed to the formation of water on Earth, with the distance of the earth from the Sun having nothing to do with the formation of water. At the formation of the earth, there is no existence of water, and it will be hard to prove how now more than 70 percent of the Earth's surface was covered with water. The emergence of water body which now covered more than 70 percent of the Earth's surface could only be possible by continuous raining, needing mammoth amount of clouds, as such would requires colossal quantity of water vapor. And if rain created the oceans, why not the Earth be covered by water even after continuous raining, having witnessing numbers of flood all over the world every year? Yet, sea level is hardly raised a centimeter. Where could the water gone?

And now, one source has claimed that scientists have discovered an animal, less than 10-celled parasite call Henneguya salminicola that lives in salmon muscle, does not need oxygen to produce energy needed for its survival-the only living organism which can live without oxygen. Another source stated, a worm-like creature which they had named Ikaria wariootia, the oldest known example of a bilaterian, which lived during the Ediacaran period dated 571 to 539 million years ago, when the first non-microscopic multicellular creatures emerged, was the ancestor of all living animals. But how true is their finding? And how should we to believe this is true? Are we going to take for granted what every science says about is true? We all know that science is changing everyday with new finding comes up almost every year. So now, if science tells us different story about how the earth came into being, should we believe that is true as well? Or if science tells us that human being is actually evolves from a panda, can we say we are descended from panda?

Science stated that, being all the living creatures not evolved or appeared at the same time, they were evolved and extinct and was then swapped by another organism where the stronger survive and the weaker make way for the stronger beings to continue and subdue the world. But who are the stronger species?

In his book, 'Origin of Species' in Chapter III, Darwin said that as more individuals are produced than can possibly survive, there must in every case be a struggle for existence, either one individual with another of the same species, or with the individuals distinct species, or with the physical condition of life. And there is no exception to the rule that every organic being naturally increases at so high a rate, that, if not destroyed, the earth would soon be covered by the progeny of a single pair. Even slow-breeding man has doubled in twenty-five years, and at this rate, in less than a thousand years, there would literally not be standing-room for his progeny. So, is that says that the stronger species should conquer the weaker species to maintain the earth in balance? Right now, it seems that human beings are the strongest species in the world in term of mentality. What stronger species will come up to check or extinct our human race?

The story of extinction of dinosaur in the face of the world is interesting as per the book of science upheld. Science maintained that the extinction of dinosaur is widely due to the eruption of volcano while some sources maintained that they were extinct due to the choking of chemical from erupting volcano and climate change. So the question is; How huge and strong is the volcano been erupted to obliterated the total inhabitants of dinosaur in one instant? Was the earth very small at that time leaving a small space for dinosaur to live together in one assemblage of land that volcano completely covered the whole land? If that is so, how comes that other organisms were able to survive such catastrophe? Why not other animal extinct together with the dinosaur? By reason, it is not possible. Wasn't the theory of science based on reason? If one or few eruptions of volcano can completely wipe out the total population of dinosaur, it can also wipe out other species but why not other species? And lately, a new theory suggested that the extinction of dinosaur might have been caused by the asteroid. Wasn't that too the same? If the asteroid could wipe out the entire population of dinosaur, why not others?

When dinosaur first existed in the world, it is said that the world is consisted of only one land mass known as Pangea and many sources stated that dinosaur live everywhere in the world for about 175 million years. That said every part of land in the world is inhabitable for dinosaur and they live every corner of the earth. The question is, how many volcanoes were erupted at that period of time that chemical released from erupting volcanoes cover the whole earth? They have adapted for about 175 million years, so how much the earth's climate has changed dramatically that it is too insensate for dinosaur to live on?

One of the most debatable questions about evolution is; how a living organism appeared from non-living thing? For as science had suggested or claimed, there were no living organisms at the time of the formation of the earth, but now, we have million kind of species living in the world today including human being. How is it possible that living organism came from non-living things and how is it possible that animal or fish of one kind transformed into some animal with wholly different structures and habits? Can you imagine a kind of fish transformed into some kind of amphibian that possess completely different structure and habits? Or just imagine how trees and plants come up differently from moving or walked organism? If every living thing in the world came from the first living organism, called prokaryotes, how is it possible that some became plants, while some become fishes and other an animals? As for me, it is ridiculous to think of a bacteria evolves into a completely differently component organism, like animals and birds with some having hair, fur and other, a feather. Should we believe that human being and can was once a fish which is evolves into two different kinds as time goes on? It is claimed that the total weight of all ants in the world is heavier than the total number of human being put together. Can we believe it because science seems to be proving it? Has they counted every single ant in the world and measure its weight? Their claim is based on assumption. And aren't we too naïve to believe in assumption it as fact?

When we stick to or rely excessively on science, we have failed to be thankful for how much different we were been created from other animals that we were able to rule this world despite of been weaker in strength and smaller in size. Comparing ourselves to elephant, bull, oxen, horse, tiger, lion etc. we stood so small and weak, however, we were able to tame or rule over them, even the strongest animal in the universe. Are not we the blessed species on this earth? How is this possible?

If we look at the word of God, Holy Bible, we can find the absolute answer. God created everything that is on Earth. He created the universe and has the knowledge of them all. God even knows how many stars He has put in the space. In Genesis chapter 1, we can find the story of the creation of the universe and of the Earth and all things that were on it. He created the Sun, the Moon, the Stars and the Earth. He created light and darkness and water and land. The plants, animals and birds that lives on land and the fishes that lives in the water.

Charles Darwin said that if not one head of game animal or birds like hare, partridges, groose etc. were not shot during the next twenty years in England, and, at the same time, if no vermin were destroyed, there would, in all probability, be less game than at present, although hundreds of thousands of game animals are now annually shot. He also said that with the elephant, none are destroyed by beasts of prey, for even the tiger in India most rarely dares attack a young elephant protected by its dam. But elephant have not overpopulated until now. Why is this possible? And how is it possible that nature generate what can be an extraordinary, a male and a female of each kind? Millions of species of living thing in the world having male and female of each kind is something impossible for nature to develop without anyone behind it. God created each species, male and female so that their kinds should reproduce their own kinds to continue to exist in the world. He created them all to depend on each other to continue its survival. God created different kind of plants and animals so that the environment of the Earth should be balance. God knows how things in the world would become so He created carnivores to check the herbivores from completely destroyed the plants and God made the life of carnivores unproductive so that they may not overturned the population of herbivores to extinction, and we called this process 'Food Chain' in science context. Science did not create this food chain to balance the environment of the earth but God did. If there are no carnivores animals in the world, what will happen to plants when the population of herbivores animal is not checked? And if the life of carnivores animals are very productive, shouldn't the lives of herbivores in danger? God has the knowledge of everything, so He created this food chain to balance the earth. And now, to whom should we be thankful for, Science or God?

From the beginning, God had created all things essential for survival before He created living things. He created animals and plants before man that man may find food when they were created. And as human being cannot live without light, He created the sun, the moon and the stars before human being and animals.

"Then God made two great lights; the greater light to rule the day, and the lesser light to rule the night: He made the stars also." Genesis 1: 16 (NKJV)

Above all creations, He created man to rule and to watch over the world. That is why we are being created very differently from other animals. He created us with the ability to think and understand. He gave us the knowledge and instilled common sense in us to understand what is good and what is bad.

Will you accept that your ancestor is developed and evolved from a single-cellular organism? When science told you that your closest ancestor is ape, are you willing to accept it because science seems so advanced? And should we give the same status to ape as to human being? At the time when there is not a single living organism exist on earth, how could a living organism came out of non-living thing? When two organisms have similar structures doesn't prove that they have same DNA.

If you look at similarity, you will certainly find that ape resembled human being the most among any other animals. But if you look at the difference, you will find thousand reasons why human cannot be the descendant of ape. Many people have blindly believes that human are directly descended from ape when science said so. Scientists tend to examine more on the similarity between human and ape while ignored the majority of dissimilarities.

We cannot take the resemblance of apes and human as the source of gene to transform from apes into human being. We should not accept the idea of man evolved from an ape because of our similarity with an ape. We are completely different from ape in jaws and teeth, skull, leg bones, foot bones, hipbones, etc. It is found out that apes tend to have incisor and canine teeth that are relatively larger than their molars and have thin enamel while humans have thicker enamel. Jaws of apes are more u-shaped while human jaws are more parabolic. The vault of the skull in human is relatively larger than that of ape. Ape and human may have some similarity but the degree of similarity doesn't mean that they have the exact function and role.

Wolf has the resemblance of dog but they were of two different kinds. Cat has some similarity with the tiger or leopard but they were different from the beginning. Boar and pig has some common congenital material in them but they were created differently from the beginning and will always remain different from each other. Likewise, we cannot be called as the descendant of apes because we have some similarity with them in hand, face, or feet. Everything in the universe except human being is created when God spoke the word. We were created differently from the beginning and not just different but with the best care and from love.

Then God said, "Let there be light": and there was light." Genesis 1: 3 (NKJV)

When God spoke the word, light appear in the universe.

Then God said, 'Let the waters under the heaven be gathered together unto one place, and let the dry land appear"; and it was so. Genesis 1: 9 (NKJV)

When God spoke the word, water and dry land separated.

Then God said," Let the earth bring forth grass, the herb that yields seed, and the fruit tree that yields fruit according to its kind, whose seed is in itself, on the earth"; and it was so. Genesis 1: 11 (NKJV)

When God spoke the word, plants and trees appeared on the earth.

Then God said, "Let there be lights in firmament of the heavens to divide the day from the night; and let them be for signs, and seasons, and for days and year; and let them be for lights in the firmament of the heaven to give light on the earth"; and it was so. Then God made two great lights; the greater light to rule the day; and the lesser light to rule the night: He made the stars also. Genesis 1: 14-16 (NKJV)

When God spoke the word, the sun, the moon and the stars appeared in the sky- the sun to rule the day and the moon to rule the night just as He says.

Then God said, "Let the waters abound with an abundance of living creatures, and let birds fly above the earth across the face of the firmament of the heaven." So God created great sea creatures and every living thing that moves, with which the waters abounded, according to their kind, and every winged bird according to its kind. And God saw that it was good. Genesis 1: 20 -21(NKJV)

When God spoke the word, fish of all kinds and birds of all kinds appeared. God blessed the water by filling different kinds of fishes, big and small, ferocious and meek. God blessed the sky with all kind of flying birds and also all kind of flying living creatures.

Then God said," Let the earth bring forth the living creature according to its kind: cattle, and creeping thing and beast of the earth, each according to its kind"; and it was so." Genesis 1: 24 (NKJV)

When God spoke the word, all kind of beast, both cattle and wild animals and reptiles appeared. He filled the land with all kind of beast, wild and domesticated. All for the benefits of man.

Then God said, "Let Us make man in Our image, according to Our likeness; let them have dominion over the fish of the sea, over the birds of the air, and over cattle, over all the earth and over every creeping thing that creeps on the earth." Genesis 1: 26 (NKJV)

And the Lord God formed man of the dust of the ground, and breathed into his nostrils the breath of life; and man became a living being. Life in God's Garden. Genesis 2: 7 (NKJV)

But when God decided to made human being, He did not just spoke the word. He formed a man from the dust of the ground and gave a breath of life that man should have a soul unlike the other living organism. And God bestow upon man the power to rule over all other living things on the earth.

Science clearly stated that a certain thing to evolve into another form takes millions of years and we understand that even if we are to believe in evolution, apes were not transformed into human being overnight leaving some apes behind to continue its ancestry line. But if apes were evolves into human being, all the apes should slowly transform into humanlike form taking millions of year together, not just some fraction among them. When something is evolve or transformed into another form, the remains of the previous form or kind is lost or destroyed as they have been transformed into something that is not them. But as we can see that we still have an apes living among us, those apes being evolved into human being as science claimed should have a different gene and have diverge lineage from that of apes seen today; because if they have the same gene, all of them should evolve together. Or if they have different gene from the beginning, both of them cannot be call or consider as one kind. For example, if human being was to evolve into another being, all of our structure, action or thinking and habit will gradually change together, irrespective of race, color and dwelling place. It ridiculous to think of only the whole populace of Europe evolves into something else while the American, the Africans or the Asian remain as it is. Or the people in the continent of Australia evolve into something else while the rest of the world remains as human being.

Instead of trying to understand the idea of evolution which some fans of science proposed, it is much better and more profitable to look into God's word because the absolute truth lies in the word of God itself. From the Holy Bible in the book of Genesis, we learned that God created beast, bird, and fish according to their kind and bless them to multiply. And God saw what He had created was good. Now let us look at the scripture.

Genesis chapter 1 verses 21 to 25 (NKJV)

So God created great sea creatures and every living thing that moves, with which the waters abounded, according to their kind, and every winged bird according to its kind. And God saw that it was good. And God blessed them, saying, "Be fruitful and multiply, and fill the waters in the seas, and let birds multiply on the earth." So the evening and the morning were the fifth day. Then God said, "Let the earth bring forth the living creature according to its kind: cattle and creeping thing and beast of the earth, each according to its kind"; and it was so. And God made the beast of the earth according to its kind, cattle according to its kind, and everything that creeps on the earth according to its kind. And God saw that it was good."

God created each species male and female to reproduce and continue their lineage in the world. They reproduce each according to their kind. And to this day, they remain as it is. No one has ever seen a lion evolve into something else. No one has ever seen a cow changed into a bison or a dog into wolf. From the beginning, a cat was a cat and to this day, it remains a cat.

Of all the created things, God did not find satisfaction in them until He created man in his likeness because all the beast or fish or bird has no common sense to praise their creator. Therefore, He created man differently from the beginning in the resemblance of Him so that we can rule or watch over what He had created. And because of this, we were able to rule over them.

Genesis chapter 1 verses 26 to 30. (NKJV)

Then God said, "Let Us make man in Our image, according to Our likeness; let them have dominion over the fish of the sea, over the birds of the air, and over the cattle, over all the earth and over every creeping thing that creeps on the earth." So God created man in His own image; in the image of God He created him; male and female He created them. Then God blessed them, and God said to them, "Be fruitful and multiply; fill the earth and subdue it; have dominion over the fish of the sea, over the birds of the air, and over every living thing that moves on the earth." And God said, "See, I have given you every herb that yields seed which is on the face of all the earth, and every tree whose fruit yields seed; to you it shall be for food. Also, to every beast of the earth, to every bird of the air, and to everything that creeps on the earth, in which there is life, I have given every green herb for food"; and it was so.

For science, they will need to explain hard why each species have male and female of their kind and what the need of their continuation in the world is. It is like asking a question on who came first; an egg or a hen?

But why did God created man in his likeness? And why does God takes special care when human being was created? God created us (man) differently from the beginning with different purpose. He created us with the ability to think and understand to glorify His creation because all the other living creatures cannot praise and glorify what He had created.

Yet, He did not created us to completely obey whatever He commanded us to do or not to do. He gave each one of us the freewill to make our own decision- to obey Him or not to obey Him. He gave each one us a CHOICE. And for this reason, we are now thinks differently and our liking differs from each other.

But in the end, there will be only one way out and those who have make the right choice will have the privilege to live in the glory of God while the rest will bear the wrath of God.

Chapter 5 Nature; Big Bang or God

Nature

Our Earth, the most beautiful planet in the Universe is home to thousands of beautiful landscape and amazing places which enthralled us by its beauty, attracting tourist from every corner of the world. The beauty of nature is by far more beautiful than the garden or park built by man and more marvellous as well. It doesn't simply happen by chances or develop from a million of years from rough rock to this beautiful landscape today with time but was designed artistically by God Himself.

Africa

African continent have the privilege to own the largest hot desert as well the longest river in the world. The Sahara desert located on the African continent is the largest hot desert in the world, covering an amazing area of 9,200,000 square kilometres. The area is approximately holds the total land area of China and United State together. And Nile River, which is 6,650 km long, is the longest river in the world. Africa also have Victoria Falls which is considered one the largest waterfalls in the world with its combined width of 1,708 meters (5604 ft). Victoria Falls is named in honour of Queen Victoria but is also known as 'Mosi-oa-Tunya' in local dialect which means 'The Smoke That Thunders' due to its thunderous sound from falling water.

Asia

The Himalaya in Asia continent has many of the Earth's highest peaks, including the Mount Everest which stood at astonishing high of 8848 meters above sea level. Asia has the largest lake in the world as well, Caspian Sea, with an area of 371,000 square kilometres. It has the Death Sea, the saltiest bodies of water in the world, which is said to be more than 9 times saltier than the ocean water. The largest natural cave in the world is also in Asia, Han Son Doong cave situated at Vietnam.

Australia

To Australia, God gave the Great Barrier Reef, the world's largest coral reef which composed of over 2,900 individual reefs and 900 islands stretching for over 2,300 kilometers (1,400 miles) over an area of approximately 344,400 square kilometers (133,000 sq. miles).

Europe

The Denmark Strait cataract is the world highest underwater waterfall with water falling almost 3,505 meters.

North America

To North America, God bestow the Gulf of Mexico, which share border with the United States, Mexico, and the island nation of Cuba, is the world's largest gulf. It has a coastline of about 5,000 kilometers (3,100 miles). The Gulf of Mexico is connected to the Atlantic Ocean by the Straits of Florida, between Cuba and the U.S. state of Florida. North America also has the Grand Canyon.

South America

South America continent has the largest river by volume in the world, Amazon River.

Angel Falls in Venezuela, which is the world's highest uninterrupted waterfall in the world, with an amazing height of 979 meters is also in South America.

God gave to each continent, a unique landscape. Only few have been mentioned in this book for information but there are thousands of splendid landscapes in every part of the world which human and scientific technology cannot build. All these land settings cannot be transformed from a mere million-year-old rusty rock.

Though science has been trying hard to explain how the nature has evolves over 4.7 billion years when the earth was first formed, the uniqueness of each landscape cannot take for granted that it was transformed from a stained rock to this beautiful landscape as the earth evolves.

If our earth works based on reason or logic, the hottest place in the world should lies around equatorial region, in the countries like Democratic Republic of the Congo, Uganda, Kenya, Somalia, Indonesia, Ecuador, Colombia or Brazil. Strange it may be but the hottest place in the world is the Death Valley in California, United State, whose highest temperature ever recorded is 56.7 degree Celsius, in the summer 1913. Death Valley has an average temperature of 47 degree and is 2503.35 miles (4028.76 kilometres) north of the Equator. When experimented on why the Death Valley was so hot, they concluded that it was due to the lack of water in the region and the area that received the maximum solar radiation. If Death Valley is so hot because there wasn't much water found in the region, why not Sahara desert which has an area about 9.2 million square kilometres the hottest place in the world where no rain is seen for several years in some parts of the desert?

Water covered about 71% of the earth's surface and about 96% of water found on earth is hold by the ocean. Despite the fact that water cannot flow upwards without the help of a motor, it amazingly does, in the form of spring. The earth is full of mysteries. And with the help of science, many secrets were been revealed. In ancient world, man does not know how spring works and why the ocean never overflows even when thousands of rivers flow into the ocean. But now, science has explained that the spring occur when the water pressure moves groundwater through the cracks and tunnels within the aquifer to the surface of the earth. And the reason why the ocean never overflows though it was fed by thousands of rivers is because water get vaporize from the water surface due to heat and the water vapour is then dry up in the air.

Have you ever imagine how spring sprout out from the earth in a high altitude like the Angel Falls which is 3212 feet above the sea level? Where do those waters come from?

Science describes the work of spring water where aquifer act as a sponge to soak up the water that seeps down into it and release it to the earth's surface as a result of a confined aquifer in which the recharge area of the spring water table rests at a higher elevation than that of the outlet. But what about the spring that flow down from the top of a mountain or a hill? If the earth was formed 4.7 billion years ago by matter of the big bang inartistically without anyone behind the creation, can you imagine that the earth is full of beautiful waterfalls, streams and rivers, valley and hills? Though science has able to find the cause of spring or ocean, it was God who designed it and how it should works. Big bang has nothing to do with how the earth should works. It was God who created thing that men and science should studies from it.

Places like Godafoss in Iceland; Playa De Las Catedrales, Spain; Dziikou Valley, India; Cliff of Moher in Ireland; Antelope Canyon, Arizona; Atacama Desert, Chile; Iguazu Falls in Argentina/Brazil; Mount Fuji, Japan; Niagara Falls, USA/Canada; Li River, China; James Bond Isaland, Thailand; Zhangjiajie National Forest Park, China; Whitehaven Beach, Australia; Lencois Maranhenses National Park, Brazil are truly magnificent. When you visit these places, you will realize how beautifully God had designed which science cannot build.

Crops and Weeds

Why do crops need care and protection while weeds do not?

Have you ever wondered why we have to labour so hard to get a good harvest?

We could have got a good harvest even without proper care and nursing if crops are growing like weeds because weeds grow very well unattended. When we planted crops, we make every possible to destroy the weeds, yet they grows up at their own will.

Imagine what our crops would become if we treated it like weeds? Can we expect a good harvest from it? If unattended, will it bear fruits? But weeds grow healthily wherever it is grown. Even insects or pests seldom destroy them while our crop is vulnerable to attack. There should be a reason behind it and it is essential to know that reason, why?

In order to have a good harvest so as to meet the requirement intake of the people around the world, science have provided different techniques for different crops. To increase the productivity of the crops, they have invented different types of fertilizers. To prevent weeds from growing along the crops, they have produced weedicide. And to control pest, they have discovered pesticides and insecticides. In order to make it easier for the farmer to raise crops, science have invented/built machine like tractor, tiller, harvester etc. Apart from the scientific technology, it is important that the farmers are equipped with the right information of practices. They need the right information of how to maintain soil fertility, for farming is not a one-year plan. They also need to know on how and when to plant crops and how to control crops pest. Even after the harvest, they would need to keep the crop away from the rodents.

Thanks to the science and technology, farming became much easier. They have the answer to every query about crops and its practices. Yet the answer on why crops need care and protection still remain in the dark.

The best answer we can find is in the Bible. At the event of the creation of the earth and humankind, God have provided everything a man would need. Everything was perfect until man disobey God, his creator. If mankind hasn't turned away from God by disobeying Him, God would still allow the earth to provide everything we would need without us toiling hard.

Read Genesis chapter 3.

Lucifer, came to the woman Eve in the form of a serpent and tempted her. She falls into his cunning words and then man fall from the grace of God when he chooses to follow his woman's footprint; to disobey God. At that very moment, the perfectness of the world was surrendered.

They disobey God by eating the fruit God had forbade them to eat when the sweet word of Lucifer was too much to resist. At this disobedient, God pronounced His judgment on all of them.

To the serpent, God cursed it to crawl on its belly and the enmity between its offspring and the woman's.

"And the Lord God said unto the serpent, because thou has done this, thou art cursed above all cattle, and above every beast of the field; upon thy belly shalt thou go, and dust shalt thou eat all the days of thy life. And I will put enmity between thee and the woman, and between thy seed and her seed; it shall bruise thy head, and thou shalt bruise his heel." - Genesis 3: 14, 15

To the woman, Eve, God punished her and her offspring by increasing the pain of childbearing and that she would be subject to her husband.

"Unto the woman he said, I will greatly multiply thy sorrow and thy conception; in sorrow thou shalt bring forth children; and thy desire shall be to thy husband, and he shall rule over thee." - Genesis 3: 16

And to man, Adam, God cursed the ground.

"And unto Adam he said, because thou hast hearkened unto the voice of thy wife, and hast eaten of the tree, of which I commanded thee saying, thou shalt not eat of it: cursed is the ground for thy sake; in sorrow shalt thou eat of it all the days of thy life. Thorns also and thistles shall it bring forth to thee; and thou shalt eat the herb of the field. In the sweat of thy face shalt thou eat bread, till thou return unto the ground; for out of it was thou taken; for dust thou art, and unto dust shalt thou return." - Genesis 3: 17

That is why, when we planted crops, it produced weeds and thistle. The land was not productive like before so that man should toil hard to get the harvest.

Men and Animals

Have you ever wonder why most of the wild beasts were active during night time and sleep during the day while human being and harmless domesticated animals sleep at night and active during the day?

Some theories related to science, postulates that most of the animals are nocturnal because this trait has evolves as a way to avoid being eaten by dinosaurs, probably during Jurassic period, and other predators for it is easier to avoid detection at night, and that these trait has remained since then.

Evolutionary biology community known as "Bottleneck Theory" also suggested that millions of years ago in the Mesozoic era, many ancestors of modern-day mammals evolved nocturnal characteristics in order to avoid contact with the numerous diurnal predators. Another hypothesis indicates that many animals are nocturnal to avoid the heat of the day.

Before dinosaur, many animals have evolved and became extinct. After dinosaur era, in Paleocene epoch, it is said that first large mammals, up to bear or small hippo size appeared, and many modern mammals appeared around 33.9 million years ago which is more than 109 million years after the extinction of dinosaur as per the geological time period based on evolution. With that said, most of the modern wild animals were evolves after the extinction of dinosaur and did not need to avoid from the assault of dinosaur. And modern predators like lion, tiger, leopard, hyena, wolf, fox and other predators did not required to evade from any other predators, but they were nocturnal by nature. Most of the diurnal animals were characteristically herbivore and harmless to other animals or domesticated. So there is no necessarily needed for nocturnal predators (carnivore animal) to stay away from any other animal during daytime.

We had also learned that animals that hunt, mate, or are generally active at night have special adaptations that make it easier to live at night. Nocturnal animals generally have highly developed senses of hearing, smell and specially adapted eyesight than the diurnal animals. They have bigger and pupil-widen eyes than the diurnal animals. Some nocturnal animals like bats hunt at night with the help of their specialized hearing, who with an extrasensory adaption use echolocation to navigate and find food by releasing a high-pitched sound that bounce off object including prey which tell the bats how far away the object and prey are, some have a good sense of smell to locate their prey/food and other have heat-sensitive sensory receptor to helps them navigate and find food.

Certain animals hibernate for months during winter when food supplies become scarce. By going into a long deep sleep, they bypass this period completely, waking up when food becomes more plentiful. It is said that during hibernation, an animal's body temperature, heartbeat, breathing and other metabolic activities slow down significantly in order to converse energy. But they do not go into hibernation at their own will. Nature itself tells them the time to go for hibernation that they may get ready for it.

We have discussed above that nocturnal animals were given specialized sense of hearing, smelling or sightedness, not by acquiring as they adapted with time. But why different animals were given different abilities?

The Holy Bible did not directly mentioned why the nocturnal animals were given the ability of seeing in the dark, specialized senses of hearing and smelling or sensitivity of heat. But God created every living being that is on Earth there is a reason why the creation has been different for each animal including human being.

And God said, Let the waters bring forth abundantly the moving creature that hath life, and fowl that may fly above the earth in the open firmament of heaven. And god created great whales, and every living creature that moveth, which the water brought forth abundantly, after their kind, and every winged fowl after his kind: and God saw it was good. And God blessed them, saying, Be fruitful, and multiply, and fill the waters in the seas, and let fowl multiply in the earth.

And God said, Let the earth bring forth the living creature after his kind, cattle, and creeping thing, and beast of the earth after his kind; and it was so. And God made the beast of the earth after his find, and cattle after their kind, and everything that creeped upon the earth after his kind: and God saw that it was good.

Genesis 1: 20-22 & 24-25 (KJV)

God created some living being to live in the water, some to fly, some animals to creeps, some to be cattle and other to be wild beasts. They did not just take their form by nature, but by the will of God. At the creation of the Earth, God put man above all creations, but with certain limitation. Just pictured what would happen if God blessed men with the ability to see in the dark like nocturnal animals and with immense power like lion or so big like elephant. It would certainly mean more harm than bringing good thing out of it. God created some animals to be herbivore and other carnivore, some to crawls and other to walks on four foot, some to creeps and other to fly. He created some animals to sleep during nighttime and some to sleep during the day. God did not simply created them to fill the earth. He gave to each of them, a purpose fitted for human being and for the earth.

God created domesticated animals to live with man during daytime while wild animals and other animals sleeps so that it would be more suitable for survival for both of them. At the very creation of the world, God gave animals to man for food and for food; men would certainly kill all the wild animals within a short span of time if they roam during the day like us or us roaming at night like them. God would not like men to annihilate what He had created from the face of the earth. Likewise, wild animals could disturb the tranquillity of man if they were active during the day. God arranged everything according to what is best for existence of each species He created.

God gave the ability of flying to the birds but He did not create any bird so big and ferocious. Can you imagine a peaceful lives if some birds were so huge and vicious? Won't they come and attack the animals, both domesticated and wild, and also human being for food like we have seen in sci-fi movie?

Have you ever wondered why every living species have male and female of each kind? When we look at science for the answer, it automatically focused to evolution, which indicated that all living beings were evolves from single-celled eukaryotic species. And from there, multicelled organism develops with time, to about 8.7 million species on earth as estimated by scientists in 2011, each species having two sexes. That means, as per evolution theory and scientific studies, all living beings were evolves from another species before them. A magnificent lion is not a lion by birth or of somebody's creation many million years ago but was evolved from a completely different animal, just as human being was evolved from an ape. What kind of being would men evolve into millions of years later?

Each species having male and female of their kind is a wonderful thing. Science may find it offensive but nature has nothing to do with their existence. All are set as God has planned. God created every living being; male and female, blessed them to multiply and fill the earth. To reproduce, God put instinct of mating into every living being. For without it, there is no other way to reproduce their offspring. If there is no instinct of mating among animals, the differentiation of being male and female would be pointless. How can an animal reproduce their progeny if they did not mate? And God makes sex pleasurable for man that they must find their partner attractive and loving. Every sane woman knew that child-bearing is painful and unpleasant, sometime referring to as 'Second Death or Next to Death' but defied it by getting married to her beloved. If we find no attraction and affection toward opposite sex, the life of human being would have been completely different. God put instinct of attractiveness, affection, fondness and love into man that he should enjoy life and also to reproduce to fulfil the will of God.

When God saw the longevity of man's life on Earth convey more of debauchedness than goodness, so numbered the lifespan of man to 120 years, and thenceforth, man did not live more than 120 years.

"And the Lord said, My spirit shall not always strive with man, for that he also is flesh: yet his days shall be an hundred and twenty years." - Genesis 6:3

Season and weather

A season is a division of the year marked by changes in weather, ecology, and amount of daylight resulting from Earth's orbit around the Sun and Earth's axial tilt relative to the ecliptic plane. Generally, we have four recognized seasons in a year; Spring Season, Summer Season, Autumn Season and Winter Season.

We have found out that as our earth is spherical and axis tilted, northern hemisphere and southern hemisphere go opposite; that is, when there is spring in the northern hemisphere, the southern hemisphere would experience autumn, and when northern hemisphere is enjoying a warm months during May, June, July and August, Southern Hemisphere would enjoy the same between December and February.

As our earth's axis tilted as it rotate by an angle of approximately 23.5 degrees and revolve around the Sun, we experience some days shorter than the other days and some days warmer than the other day throughout the year. When the North Pole tilts toward the Sun, it is summer in the Northern Hemisphere and winter in the Southern Hemisphere. Likewise, it is summer in Southern Hemisphere and winter in Northern Hemisphere when the South Pole tilts toward the Sun. We will have no season if our Earth doesn't tilt its axis.

Science explained the reason of having different season in a year is due to the Earth spins on its axis and move around the sun in elliptical orbit taking 365 days to complete one revolution around the sun. From the book of science, we learn that the earth's axis is an invisible line that runs through its centre, from pole to pole. We can observe the effect of axial tilt of the earth as the length of days and altitude of the sun at noon changes during a year. During winter, the low angle of the sun makes the light received by the Earth more indirect and of low intensity than during summer. That is why we experience a cold winter.

Yet the seasons are not the result of the variation in Earth's distance to the sun because of its elliptical orbit. We do not know how far it is true but it is said that the Sun is closest to the Earth during Northern Hemisphere's winter. Thus, the amount of sunlight heating the Earth should be more intense during winter than summer but the northern hemisphere experience a warmer summer.

From the Holy Bible, we know that God created and position the earth at the very best place and how the earth must have different season throughout the year.

In Genesis 1: 14, God said, "Let there be lights in the firmament of the heavens to divide the day from the night; and let them be for signs and seasons, and for days and years."

Here, God did not simply say that the earth will have day and night because of the sun and the moon. We all know that without the revolution of the earth will have no winter or summer and there will be no year at all with only day and night. We are able to count year by its one complete revolution round the sun but how will we count year and time if the earth just spins on its axis without revolve round the sun? God created the earth and the universe in such a way that the earth should have seasons and years.

Weather

In general term, weather is the state of the temperature, describing the degree to which it is hot or cold, wet or dry, calm or stormy, clear or cloudy. Weather refers to day-to-day temperature and precipitation activity. Weather occurs due to air pressure, temperature and moisture differences between one place to another.

The practice of forecasting weather has been known as early as 650 BC by the Babylonian who used cloud patterns and astrology to predict the weather. About 300 years later, Aristotle described weather patterns in Meteorologica followed by Theophrastus in his book 'Book of Signs'. Then the Chinese and Indian developed weather prediction method in about 300 BC. The ancient weather forecasting method relied on observed patterns of events of the sky. The modern weather forecast began in 1835 with the invention of Electric Telegraph. On August 1, 1861 saw the first ever daily weather forecasts which were published in 'The Times'.

Now, Barometer, the most commonly used weather forecasting instrument is invented by Italian Physicist and Mathematician Evangelista Torricelli, who was a student of Galileo in 1643. The used of barometer in predicting the weather become more precise and helped people aware of bad weather before its coming. Many lives were been saved by the warning of severe weather like tornado, hurricane, typhoon, tsunami etc. by the meteorological department, thanks to the invention of barometer before the harsh weather comes. However, the advancement of technology has made people questioned about involvement of God in our lives. And many great scientists had even claimed that there is no God.

Science has taught us that we experience different seasons because of the Earth spin on its axis and due to the elliptical orbit around the sun. But seasons doesn't simply change with the earth's axis tilted or elliptical orbit around the sun as nature itself demanded. Science tells us what and how but never who. Science tells us the creation of the universe through the Big Bang but have you ever re-examined why the Sun stood still while the planets and the stars orbit around the sun? Does the Big Bang have prior knowledge about how the universe should function according to plan?

When I study about the Big Bang, these questions keep roving in my head;

Why does the Earth spin on its axis without changing its course or direction aimlessly even after spinning for thousands and thousands of years?

Why doesn't the Earth move faster or slower sometime?

Why the Earth always revolves around the sun without straying out of its track?

What force makes the earth spinning?

What force makes the earth orbiting the sun?

Science enlightened us that the Earth orbit around the sun without straying from its track is due to magnetic field of the sun. But was that enough an answer? Something must have causes that magnetic field, and what was that?

Then, I find something that is very interesting as well as done with my doubt. I look to God and He shows me the answer I was searching for. God has planned everything about the universe was created. At the time of God created the light, He has design how our universe should work. And God said, "Let there be lights in the firmament of the heaven to divide the day from the night; and let them be for signs, and for seasons, and for days, and years."

Genesis 1: 14 (KJV)

God knows that without the turning or spinning of the Earth, there won't be day and night. So He made the Earth spin, not only to spin randomly, but on its axis, because an ununiformed movement or spinning of the Earth would disturb the lives on the Earth. God made the Earth elliptically orbit the Sun and its axis titled because the Earth standing upright and doesn't orbit the sun would mean there will be no seasons at all. God made only one Sun to gives light as well as heat out of thousands of stars and planets, because having two or more object like the sun that produce heat would burn out our Earth which will made unfavourable for living.

How would you feel if you have only one season throughout the year round, I mean all your life? Can it be enjoyable to have only summer or winter all your life? There's time for everything under heaven just as God had planned. Nature did not simply allow things to happen arbitrarily. To everything, God set a time and it happened at the time He chooses.

With the advancement of technology, the prediction of weather becomes more precise, and this makes people put their faith towards scientific technology. But God chooses when to. Many a time we have seen an unexpected harsh weathers and natural disasters and also avert from severe weather forecast. A human's projection (scientific weather forecast) is based on scientific calculation but it is God who controls everything. He can make things happen without warning or divert or stop anything from happening.

When God destroyed the Earth with flood during the time of Noah, the flood or the rain did not just happened accidentally. Before He brings flood, God had warned the people from sinning to avoid facing the consequences. But when the people refuses to obey God and keeps on sinning, God finally decided to completely wipe out the people from the face of the earth.

"And God saw that the wickedness of man was great in the earth, and that every imagination of the thoughts of his heart was only evil continually. And it repented the Lord that He had made man on the earth, and it grieved Him at heart. And the Lord said, I will destroy man whom I have created from the face of the earth; both man, and beast, and the creeping thing, and the fowls of the air; for it repented me that I have made them."

Genesis 6: 5-7

"And, behold, I, even I, do bring a flood of waters upon the earth, to destroy all flesh, wherein is the breath of life, from under heaven, and everything that is in the earth shall die." Genesis 6: 17

How sinful world it is that God find only Noah's family righteous and worthy to be saved on Earth. To save the mankind, God instructed Noah to build an ark to survive the flood that mankind should flourish again through Noah. And God allowed not a single drop of rain fall on the land of Israel for three years during the time of his prophet Elijah when He is angry.

When it was necessary, God had even put the Earth to halt until Joshua and his men defeated the Amorites.

Then Joshua spoke to the Lord in the day when the Lord delivered up the Amorites before the children of Israel, and he said in the sight of Israel: "Sun, stand still over Gibeon; And Moon, in the Valley of Aijolon". So the sun stood still, And the moon stopped, Till the people had revenge Upon their enemies. Is this not written in the Book of Jasher? So the sun stood still in the midst of heaven, and did not hasten to go down for about a whole day. And there has been no day like that, before it or after it, that the Lord heeded the voice of a man; for the Lord fought for Israel.

Joshua 10: 12- 14 (NKJV)
This clearly shows that nature works at the command of God. Scientific predictions may come true sometime because they also predicted after much studies and researches. People tends to praise science when their prediction comes true, but when it did not come as foretold, men take for granted that their calculation might have gone wrong; never wanted to admit the involvement of God in their lives.
Be it rain or rainbow or wind, thunder or lightning, tornado or earthquake or volcano, science had invented instruments to study about them. With it, we come to know that rain fall to Earth after water droplets condense onto one another within the cloud causing the droplets to grow and gets too heavy to stay suspended in the cloud. When you search on Google about why wind blows, you will find that the uneven heating of the Earth's surface by the sun causes wind. It is said that rainbow is caused by reflection, refraction and dispersion of light in water droplets resulting in a spectrum of light appearing in the sky taking the form of a multicoloured circular arc. Source

from National Geographic said that lightning is caused by imbalances between storm clouds and the ground, or within the cloud themselves. Lightning is so hot that it can heat the air around it to temperatures five times hotter than the sun's surface. Science or dictionary defined an earthquake as the shaking of the surface of the Earth, resulting from the sudden release of energy in the Earth's lithosphere that creates seismic waves due to the sudden breaks of underground rocks along a fault or sudden slip on a fault.

All these explanations though in brief were made available by the advancement of science and its technology. To study the nature, man built machine. When we get almost all the answer through science, we should not get carried away by it. We should also know that science is a creation of man to study the nature and worshipping science is just like worshipping an idol we had shaped.

Have you ever wondered why we experienced heavy downpour during May, June and July or feel the wrath of wind in spring? Wasn't it a wonderful sight to see a perfect semi-circular arc rainbow of seven-coloured? Why we never saw them in different shape? Science may have invented different kinds of instruments to study the formation of clouds, the speed of wind, or the kind of weather the world would relish at certain time or place or anything related to nature, but everything under heaven works at the command of God. With their technologies, they might be able to create mini earthquake, mini rainbow, mini gusty wind, mini tornado, mini rainfall, but they cannot prevent or stop earthquake, tsunami, tornado, volcano or wind from causing disaster. When God chooses to destroy certain thing, no power and machine on earth can prevent it.

I set My rainbow in the cloud, and it shall be for the sign of the covenant between Me and the earth. It shall be, when I bring a cloud over the earth, that the rainbow shall be seen in the cloud; and I will remember My covenant which is between Me and you and every living creature of all flesh; the water shall never again become a flood to destroy all flesh. - Genesis 9:13-15 (NKJV)

Rainbow did not just appear in the sky by chances. God allow nature to make it appear after shower.

In the book of Number 16:28-33, Moses said to the Israelite when Korah, Dathan and Abiram and their men rebelled against Moses and Aaron;

And Moses said: "By this you shall know that the Lord has sent me to do all these works, for I have not done them of my own will. If these men die naturally like all men, or if they are visited by the common fate of all men, then the Lord has not sent me. But if the Lord creates a new thing, and the earth opens its mouth and swallows them up with all that belongs to them, and they go down alive into the pit, then you will understand that these men have rejected the Lord." Now it come to pass, as he finished speaking all these words, that the ground split apart under them, and the earth opened its mouth and swallowed them up, with their households and all the men with Korah, with all their goods. So they and all those with them went down alive into the pit, the earth closed over them, and the perished from among the assembly.

God opened up the earth and let it devour the men when He chooses to.

When God became angry, He allows it to rain for forty days and nights to let water cover the whole land. And He

made wind to pass over the earth to blow away the water. For complete story, please read Genesis 6, 7 and 8.
At His command, the wind can change it direction or the rain withdraw its course just as God allow the sun stood still until the Israelite defeated the Amorites and divided the Jordan River for the people of Israel to cross the river on dry ground in the days of Joshua.

Chapter 6 Calamity And God

Why Does God Allow Bad Things to Happen to good people or his followers?

Natural calamities and disasters claimed thousands of people and hundreds more lives were taken by accidents every year. When such disasters and accidents happened to the Christian, questions were been asked on why the loving and all-powerful God would allow such bad thing to happen to His followers.

This world is not a safe place anymore after sin creeps in. Before sin stained the earth, everything was very good and man live in fellowship with God where misery, pain, suffering, sadness, and death were not known to man but after sin enter the world, all kind of evils fills the earth and God punish man for their disobedience; with suffering and death.

As human population rises, so are tragedies, accidents, calamities. While at some place seems to be normal at a moment, somewhere in other part of the world saw death. And we cannot assure ourselves that nothing would happen to us. We might be shot at all of a sudden by somebody. We might meet with an accident while we enjoy our lives. Or natural calamity might fall upon us when we expected least. Though Christians were called God's people, they still were not safe.

When disaster hits the people, Christian weren't leave alone unharmed. They shared the same misfortune together with the unbelievers. There is no guarantee that a faithful Christian won't suffer chronic diseases. There is no assurance of peace for those who believe in Jesus Christ. Instead, they were been persecuted for being the follower of Christ.

The world is becoming obsessed with or was dragged by the thoughts of wickedness, ready to hurl at when situation arises. And those lesser mouth becomes the victim of the oppressor. When Christian suffered, non-believer hurled question at them, 'Where is your God?' They challenged the supremacy and existence of God that if God really existed and is all-powerful and all-loving, He won't allow such bad thing happen to His followers. And when such questions were been asked, many Christians who weren't well acquainted with the word of God or wasn't fully taught about their God, failed to give satisfactory answer to the questioners. But there is an answer to every question asked.

Atheists were reluctance in the acceptation of God as the creator or the master over every creation or created things when, in their view, saw no differences been set between the believer and non-believer at lives, in which they saw the suffering of Christian at the hand of natural calamity, misfortune, and other adversity just as non-believers do. Miseries does not leaving the Christian alone. That is why, they thought believing in Christian's God has no advantage over the unbelievers. And they questioned themselves, "Why should I follow God/Jesus if nothing special is given or treated for being his follower?"

God has the absolute authority over the earth, which

means that He can do anything in the way He wishes to. And He could force us to do only what He demanded, but He created human being and gave the gift of freewill; to choose and to make one's own decision, and to enjoy one's own dignity of freewill. He did not force you to do anything whether good or bad. Therefore, whether to be good or bad is in your hand. Whether to have a good relationship with Him or to reject Him is at your own will. But the difference is the reward and the punishment. And it is your own freewill whether to receive reward or punishment that you cannot blame on anybody else in the end.

God did not promise an easy life for his followers. In Matthew 24: 6, Jesus said to His disciple that they will be persecuted and be handed over to be killed, and that all the nations will hate them for His namesake. It happened around the world just as He had said earlier. Christians were being persecuted and many have lost their life for their faith. But why does Christian still keep their faith despite all the hardships? Christian believes that the glory of keeping the faith is preserve for them in heaven which is to be rewarded on the judgment day.

Jesus did not call the people to believe in God and in Him that whosoever believes will have trouble-free and painless life. He rather plainly told them that they will be persecuted for believing in God. But His word did not end there. While He warned about the trouble for being His follower, He also promised about eternal life to whosoever stands his faith firm to the end.

And as God know what man is; arrogant, selfish and conceited, He allows calamity and difficulty to happen to the people so that the people will not say "We are the greatest of all thing on earth." For when life becomes too easy for the people, where sadness, miseries and troubles were not found, man will automatically take life for granted and will become conceited, forget their creator and declare themselves superior over all things, and only to be claim themselves as god.

God allows difficult time to ensue on His faithful followers as well but that doesn't mean He had forgotten them. At every difficulty, there is always hope and strength that God provides, because He did not want them to be crushed completely. He gave strength to those who love Him that they will not be vanished alongside the unbelievers when hardship comes. And Christian believes in their God because God is bigger than all the trouble that can strike them. No matter how great the trouble is, they knew that their God will not forsake them. The best example we can find is in Apostle Paul's second letter to the Corinthian Church.

"We are troubled on every side, yet not distressed; we are perplexed, but not in despair; Persecuted, but not forsaken; cast down, but not destroyed."

2 Corinthians 4: 8 &

9 (KJV)

Jesus plainly told us (in the book of Matthew) that He did not come unto this earth to bring peace but division.

"Think not that I am come to send peace on earth: I came not to send peace, but sword. For I am come to set a man at variance against his father, and daughter against her mother, and daughter in law against her mother in law. And a man's foes shall be they of his own household."

Matthew 10: 34- 36

Many of us think that if Jesus is God, He should have conquered the evil and rule this world with justice because He can do anything in his liking. And people questioned; "Why would Jesus died in the hand of His enemy if He is God?"

'Was He actually not God as He claimed He is? And if He did not come to bring peace, why did He come?'

"What is the benefit of his coming if He came to set a man against another man?"

While we find fault in others, we forget to correct ourselves the fault which is in us. Jesus came with the greatest purpose that no man could execute. If He were come to rule this earth, He can and He will because He can. But, contrary to our judgment, the purpose of His coming is to die for the world, and He did die for all of us so that we all may be saved. During the time of Jesus living on earth, people did try to make Him their king but He escaped from them because He knew He did not come to the earth to be king.

But why did He came to set a man against another man? His own son? Her own daughter? Jesus said so, because He already knew that father will go against his son for believing in Him. He already knew that a day will come when all the people will go against those who follow Him. That is why He told us that whoever loves his father or mother more than Him is not worthy to be call his disciple because those people will forsake Him when hardship comes.

"He that loveth father or mother more than me is not worthy of me: and he that loveth son or daughter more than me is not worthy of me. And he that taketh not his cross, and followed after me, is not worthy of me."

Matthew 10: 37 & 38
God allows his follower to experience calamity because it is His desire to let the people experience His strength. He wants us to rely on Him and to honour Him. And, behind every hardship, there is always a reward. When Jesus talked about the hardship, He also talked about the reward each man would receive according to his deeds. That is why; Christians were ready to endure all kind of hardships and difficulties that they may receive the reward as promised.
Then Jesus said to all of us:
"Come unto, all ye that labour and are heavy laden, and I will give you rest."

Matthew 11: 28
We may think we did nothing too odious to deserve the suffering and the pain we faced. Likewise, we may think he or she did not deserve what was happening to him or her. But God's plan is always better than we imagine and there is nothing we can do to go against Him. Sometime, we face difficulties as a punishment for our sin. And sometime, difficulties come to test our faith in Him and at other time, it came to strengthen our faith. And the reward of passing the test is always beautiful and sweet.
Look at Job story.
God Himself declared Job as the most faithful devotee of Him in the whole world.
Then the Lord said to Satan, "Have you considered My servant Job, that there is none like him on the earth, a blameless and upright man, one who fears God and shuns evil?"

Job 1: 8 (NKJV)

Then Satan questioned God if Job would still worship God when he got nothing at all, and said that God had always blessed and protected Job and his family and everything that he own. Satan doubted Job's faith and said that he would curse God if everything he owned is taken away. Like Satan, most of the people in the world consider God should protect and give prosperity to those who worship Him. God had no doubt about Job and allow Satan to test him.

And the Lord said to Satan, "Behold, all that he has is in your power, only do not lay a hand on his person." So Satan went out from the presence of the Lord. Job1:12

Then Satan destroyed all the wealth of Job and his children but to his amazement, Job said,

And he said, "Naked I came from my mother's womb, And naked shall I retuned there. The Lord gave, and the Lord has taken away; Blessed be the name of the Lord."

Job 1: 21 (NKJV)

And in spite of everything that had happened, Job did not sin by blaming God.

God allow Job to be tested by Satan again. Satan made sores break out all over Job's body. When his wife could not able see the pain he endured, she advised her husband to curse God and die.

But he said to her, "You speak as one of the foolish women speaks. Shall we indeed accept good from God, and shall we not accept adversity" In all this Job did not sin with his lips.

Job 2:10 (NKJV)

Job kept his faith unto God, had endure the worst to the end without complaining, and at the end, God blessed him double-fold than he was blessed before. Job is the only man on earth to receive the double blessing from God.

Abraham was tested to offer his only son as a sacrifice to God. When his God told him to, he obeyed. He was ready to do anything God had said. Read Genesis 22 verses 1 to 19. And because of his faith, he was called 'Friend of God'.

Joseph was sold by his own brothers, yet he held no grudge feeling toward his brothers. He was tempted by his master's wife to sleep with her. He overcome the temptation, endured the hardship in the dungeon and went on to become the Prime Minister of Egypt.

King David refused to kill his enemy (Saul) whom God had anointed the king of His people in spite of been severely persecuted by King Saul. He went on to become the greatest king of Israel.

God did not spare his most faithful followers from troubles. God even allow Satan to tempt Jesus Christ, His only son. And Jesus Christ set an example to all men when He died on the cross for us that no man can escape pain and suffering but He also shows that there is sweetness in the victory of such difficult time. And whosoever believes in God and in Jesus Christ will be saved and have eternal life in heaven.

Misfortune and the Follower of Jesus Christ

Let me tell you a story: Jones was a faithful follower of Jesus Christ. He has a friend, Martin who was an atheist. They both love football so they often played together after class. Jones wants his friend to be a believer like him, therefore preached the words of God to his friend whenever time fits. Martin won't say a word as if considering of becoming a follower of Jesus like Jones. Their college had a tournament and unfortunately, their team was defeated in the final. Before the commencement of the game, Martin saw his friend Jones praying to God and he thought Jones's prayer had failed. Then a month after, Jones's parents were killed in a car accident which is followed by another misfortune; his house was completely demolished by fire. Yet all these misfortunes, Jones did not lose his faith in his Lord Jesus Christ which surprises his friend Martin.

Martin became a manager in a reputed company where Jones serves as a security guard. One day, Martin said to Jones over a cup of tea, "You Christian claimed that your Jesus Christ is the son of God which means that he is God as well. It is said that your God is merciful and compassionate as well as holy and all-powerful. Well then, if anyone faithfully serves Jesus Christ, he/she should have all the good things in the world. God should have given his faithful followers riches, fame, long life because He will lose nothing by giving them away. On the contrary, I see the followers of Christ struggling in their life. They were generally poor, for all the wealthy people in the world do not believe in God. They helped themselves getting rich. If God wants the people to be his follower, he should give them generously whatever they want. If he cannot give it, who would want to follow a miser God? And why would your God allow such a misfortune befall on his faithful follower like you? Your God is not merciful and he doesn't know how to please his followers. I did not worship him and yet I'm prosperous and no bad thing happens to me. I will not follow him. Why don't you curse him and be like

me?"
It was Jones this time who did not say a word. He just pray silently to give him strength to go on. Like Martin, most atheists put the same question on Christianity, "Why would God allow such misfortune ensue on his faithful worshippers if He is holy and merciful God?" They wanted the best life in the world.
Wicked as we are, we wanted only the good thing. We are happy when everything goes well with us and cursed the day bad thing happen to us. We are glad when we get something and complaint when something is taken away from us.
In atheist term, 'Love those who loves you and hate those who hates you.' They questioned, "If God allow me to fail and help my enemy, why should I serve him?" We love serving a man who is generous, somebody who is kind to us.
However, for Christian, Jesus advice the other way. In Mathew 5:43-48, He told his disciples to love their enemy and pray for those who persecuted them. In earthly context, loving one's own enemy is futile, for an enemy will do nothing good to a person. And praying for those who persecuted us is meaningless, for they are the very people who were trying to destroy us. There is no reward for loving an enemy and praying for those who persecuted us. But the reward God would give is different. And that is the greatest reward a person would receive. The Reward of Life in Heaven.
In verse 46, Jesus said, "If you love those who love you, what reward will you get? Are not even the tax collectors doing that?"

Yes! Even the worst criminal loves those who love him. And if we speak or pray only for our friend, we did nothing extraordinary, for even an outlaw person speak for his friend.

When we talk about riches, we have a propensity on referring to earthly riches from where we can get respect and honor. We do not want to be poor in the eyes of the people around us. We do not want to be taken lightly by the people for being poor. We want praises and appreciations in this world. And when somebody is getting better of us, we have the tendency to get jealous over the person.

However, what God offer riches for us is different. In Mathew 6: 19-21, we are told not to store up riches on earth where moths and rust can destroy and robbers can steal it. Yes! The riches we had earned for is not permanent. No matter how rich we are, we have a limited time to enjoy it. Those wealth we toiled so hard for, cannot be taken along with us when we die. After death, this riches would mean nothing to us at all.

We are advice to store up riches in heaven where moth and rust cannot destroy and robbers cannot steal it. For that is where real life we are going to enjoy if we are worthy member to be there.

And there are only two ways and two options for us, whether to serve God even if it is hard or the earthly riches. To go through the narrow gate or the broad gate; the narrow gate that lead to life (heaven) or the broad gate that lead to death (hell). Jesus plainly told us that the narrow gate is hard and the broad gate is easy. It is our choice whether to take the easy way or the hard way.

Choosing the easy way, we will have easy life here on earth

where no one would persecuted us for being somebody's followers; enjoy the riches we had earned so hard for, at least before we die; doing what we like whether it's good or bad, at least good to us before we die; enjoy the pleasure the world provides, at least before we die; what to happen after death, we leave it behind. Choosing the easy way, we readily and intentionally offer ourselves to hell where we will spend eternally in unquenchable flame. But remember! The moment we landed in hell, there is no turning back and no repentance acceptable.

Choosing the hard way, we willingly and intentionally accepted to be persecuted for being somebody's follower, only in this short life on earth. We allow ourselves to live a simple life here on earth, only before we die; agreed to do only what God commanded to do whether it is pleasant or not, only before we die; accepted to suffer what the world would do to us, only before we die; whatever happen after death, we leave it to God. Choosing the hard way or the narrow gate, we offer our life completely to God. But remember! Suffer in this wicked world for a short time, please to do what God commanded to do is thousands fold better than living a beautiful life on earth and ends up going to hell. For we will go to heaven to live eternally where no sorrow and suffering will be seen.

Jesus also plainly told us that we cannot serve two masters at a time. In Mathew 6:24, "No one can serve two masters. Either he will hate the one and love the other, or he will be devoted to the one and despise the other. You cannot serve both God and money"

There is only one choice to make, either to serve God or money. To serve God, we choose to go through the hard way or the narrow gate. And choosing money, we accepted the broad gate and easy way of life. To serve God, we accepted to enjoy or suffer what is store for us. So when persecution comes, we must not turn back to choose the broad gate. We must not complaint thereafter why you're allowed to suffer while your friend enjoy life.

In Mathew 10: 34, Jesus had clearly told us that He did not come to bring peace to the world as most people think he would but sword. The following verse read, "For I have come to turn a man against his father, a daughter against her mother, a daughter-in-law against her mother-in-law. A man's enemies will be the members of his own household."

Why did He said that? If He came to set a son against his father and daughter against his mother, is there a good point of his coming? And what is mean by that? Was not He came into the world to save sinners (people)?

Yes! He came to save the sinners, and for that, He died on the cross for us. So then, why would He cause sons to go against their fathers and daughters against their mothers?

Jesus knew of the coming persecution on his followers. He knew that the heathen (unbeliever) would persecute his followers for believing in Him and preaching the good news about salvation. That happens even before His death. He was been persecuted by the Pharisees and Scribes for preaching the good news about the kingdom of God.

In Mathew 10: 16- 22, he said to his disciples, "Behold, I send you out as sheep in the midst of wolves. Therefore be wise as serpents and harmless as doves. But beware of men, for they will deliver you up to councils and scourge you in their synagogues. You will be brought before governors and kings for My sake, as a testimony to them and to the Gentiles. But when they deliver you up, do not worry about how or what you should speak. For it will be given to you in that hour what you should speak; for it is not you who speak, but the Spirit of your Father who speaks in you. Now brother will deliver up brother to death, and a father his child; and children will rise up against parents and cause them to be put to death. And you will be hated by all for My name's sake. But he who endures to the end will be saved."

Jesus Christ did not mean to say that His coming was deliberate to cause son against father and daughter against mother. What he means is that, as mentioned earlier, men will hate his own son for believing in Him. We should not be surprise but what he had foretold began to come true. Christians were been persecuted everywhere. Father kills his sons for believing in Jesus Christ. Daughters were been put to death for being the follower of Jesus. But the good news is, Jesus had promised that whoever lost his/her life for the sake of Him will be saved.

Jesus did not promise His followers the good thing of the world. He rather told them that they would suffer for His sake. It is clearly written in the scripture, Mathew 16: 24 that Jesus said, "If anyone would come after me, he must deny himself and take up his cross and follow me."

Jesus doesn't mean his followers should carry the cross just like He did. The cross mentioned here is about the suffering and persecution they must bear for being the follower of Jesus.

In Mathew 10: 37, Jesus also said, "He who loves his father or mother more than Me is not worthy of Me. And he who loves his son or daughter more than me is not worthy of Me. And he who does not take his cross and follow Me is not worthy of Me." and in verse 28, He said, "And do not fear those who kill the body but cannot kill the soul. But rather, fear Him who is able to destroy both soul and body in hell."

Therefore, if we are to follow Jesus, we must not be afraid when our father or mother orders us to stop worshipping Him. Christian should not be afraid those who persecuted them. They may kill us for following Jesus and preaching the words of God but they cannot kill our soul. We may be humiliated in the public but the reward which is store for us is even greater than the shame the world can give.

Chapter 7 Is God Unfair

When the argument about God deepened, atheist generally asked: If God is just, kind and merciful as Christian claimed, why is He unfair? Why is there a high and low in us? Was not He made partiality when He made me ugly and somebody very beautiful and handsome? Why did He make me born into a poor family while he from rich family? Why did He make me dark and she fair? Why is her voice so sweet while mine's not? There are many more questions atheist asked, trying to put God at guilty at certain point.

It is quite true that men are all different. Some are made famous why other don't. Somebody a millionaire and other a pauper. Some persons are beautiful and some persons ugly, strong: weak, fair: dark, wise: foolish, big: small, etc. Somebody were made master over another person.

Many thought they were right to complaint against God for making them inferior to somebody. The wisdom of God is beyond our understanding. He made everything differently for different purposes.

Look at the potter! From the same lump of clay, he made pot of different size, style and for different purposes and occasions. It is his choice whether to make it small or big, for special occasion or just ordinary uses. Does the clay have the right to compliant against its maker?

Look at the carmaker! It is his or their choice whether to

make it economy car or family car; sport car or sedan. Doesn't the maker have the power and the right to manufacture in their liking?

Different part of organs makes a human body. No (single) part of it can call a whole body without the other organs. The eyes cannot say to the ears, 'we don't need you!', or the nose cannot complaint why it did not make as a mouth. Even the hair which we think not important is needed in the human body. No individual part of a body can live on its own.

For now, let us assume that God have made all men equal in every spheres; all men rich, handsome, strong and famous. If God have make all men rich, who is there to appreciate of being rich and feel the agony of being poor? Likewise who will be appreciated of being handsome? If God gave each man the same accent of voice, who is left to appreciate the sweet melody of a song?

If everybody is as wise as anybody else, who is there to appreciate of being wise? And if God gave each man the same talent, facet, riches or power, the world would certainly be in chaos. For this reason, God created all men different with different talent and purposes so as to live interdependent.

Let's say, God gave all the people in the world the same talent in football. When all man play football, who will feed them if there was not farmer to produce rice and other crops? Or, let's say, a football team has 11 men with the same skill, be it Cristiano Ronaldo or Lionel Messi. Will it work? Can a team comprising of 11 Messi the best XI in the world? He is one of the best strikers in the world, he may adapt himself at mid or wing, but can you imagine him playing at defense or goalie? A team is not about a single position. Every team required a goal-keeper, defenders, mid-fielders, wingers and forwards. Similarly, the world is at best when different talents work together for the good of the people.

We all knew that no man is perfect. No man have the ability to do all things or able to live perfectly by his own. No matter how rich, wise or powerful he is, he needed somebody to fill his needs. Even a sick man is needed for somebody else; for without them, doctor would be of no use. Doctor need sick person to run their profession and in turn a sick person need doctor to cure their sickness. Likewise, the richest man in the world need farmer to provide food for his stomach. If there is no food which is supplied by farmer, what is the use of having all the money in the world?

It is very surprising thing that even a crime and dispute is useful to somebody. You may think that crime is not at all good and not at all necessary. If you were a lawyer, what would you do if no crime is committed at all and no case is filed over a dispute then? Won't being a lawyer, meaningless if there were no crime at all? However, that doesn't mean that a crime has a good cause to our life.

No other man can match a car maker in making car, yet he can never compete a lawyer in solving a dispute. No other man can compete footballers in playing a football match, but a footballer cannot match a swimmer in swimming competition. Likewise, no other man can match a dancer in dancing however they cannot compete an architect in the architecture field. No other man can match a scientist in the scientific field however, how wise and brilliant they may be, they can never compete a singer in singing competition.

God gave each man a unique talent. To some, he gave the ability to make somebody laugh, to others; He gave the ability to sing. To somebody, He gave the ability to write and to some, He gave the talent of acting. To somebody, He gave the talent of thinking and to some, the talent of counseling.

God made somebody beautiful and He gave somebody good health. He gave somebody riches and gave somebody long life. Look into yourself and you will be surprise to find that God has given you a talent which your friend does not have. Look down at self, discouraging of being poor, ugly, inferior is not a good idea. Being beautiful doesn't mean they will have a perfect marriage. Being rich doesn't guarantee a happiness. Being powerful doesn't guarantee a victory or freedom.

Just as proverbs says, "All that glitter is not gold" all that is beautiful is not good. A person might look so pretty, but insides, most of them are either has bad temper, lousy, ignorance, or boastful. Being the richest person in the world doesn't mean he is the most successful man in the world. He may either lack happy family, long life, or good health.

Albert Einstein maybe one of the greatest physicists of all time but not everyone appreciate his works. Some may even don't want to know about him. Xi Jingping maybe one of the most powerful men in the world right now but not everybody likes him or wants to be him. Frances Bernard Arnault maybe the one of the richest person in the world but somebody might don't want to be like him. Bella Hadid maybe one of the most beautiful women in the world but there may be some person who doesn't wants to be like her. Cristiano Ronaldo maybe one of the best footballers in the world but not everybody wants to be him. Therefore, no one can claim himself the most successful person in the world. No one can claim himself the best in the world either. And God made no partiality to anything or to anybody.

Chapter 8 Technology And God

The discovery of modern science has changed the face of the world. Even the invention of simple safety pin changed the lifestyle of human race. Some of the earliest invention that science can boast about has been made thousands of years ago. Having almost all the thing we need been invented, Charles H. Duell made his famous quote that says, “Everything that can be invented has been invented” in 1902 which turned out to be incorrect as after his famous quotation, many more wonderful and better inventions comes to light.

Without the invention of what we see and heard today, the world would still be like hundred years back from today. No man can deny almost all the inventions were making it possible by science. With it, the learning of science and its subject became one of the most prestigious professions in the world.

Science has been a blessing to the world, although it has its setback as well. Let us look at some inventions which change the primitive world to the modernize world we see today.

1. Wheel: The inventor is not known, and it is believes invented around 3400 BC by the Mesopotamians.

2. Banknote: The first banknote were in used in China during the Tang and Song dynasties, starting in the 7th century making it easier for men in commercial

transactions. And now, cashless payment makes even more comfortable and easier to use.

3. Mechanical clock: It was invented in 725 AD in China by Yi Xing and Liang Lingzan.

4. Gunpowder: Gunpowder is believed to be invented and was in used in China during the Tang Dynasty in 9th century.

5. Numerical zero: Numerical zero is invented by Indian Mathematician Aryabatta in 9th century.

6. Ambulance: Ambulance was invented by the Crusaders in Palestine and Lebanon in 11th century.

7. Eyeglass: Eyeglass is invented in Italy in 1286.

8. Printing Press: Printing press is invented in 1439 by Johannes Gutenberg.

9. Newspaper: Newspaper is first published in Korea in 1577.

10. Telescope: The actual inventor of telescope is unknown. Hans Lippershey was credited as the inventor of telescope in 1908, while some claimed that it was Galileo Galilei who invented it.

11. Mechanical calculator. The first mechanical calculator 'The Pascaline' is invented by Blaise Pascal in 1642.

12. Pendulum clock: Pendulum clock is invented by Christiaan Huygens in 1656.

13. Piston Engine: Christiaan Huygens was thought to be the inventor of piston engine as he provides the first known description of a piston engine in 1680.

14. Steam engine: Thomas Newcomen built the first commercial steam engine in 1712.

15. Spinning machine: Lewis Paul and John Wyatt invented the first mechanized cotton spinning machine in 1738.

16. Electricity: Electricity is thought to be first discovered by Benjamin Franklin in 1752.
17. Refrigerator: William Cullen invented the first artificial refrigeration machine in 1755. And in 1843, Jacob Parkins built the first practical refrigerator.
18. Carbonated water: Joseph Priestley invents a method for the production of carbonated water in 1767.
19. Car: Nicolas-Joseph Cugnot invented car in 1767.
20. Weighing scale: Richard Salter invented the earliest known weighing scale in 1770.
21. Boring machine: John Wilkinson invented boring machine in 1774 which is considered by some to be the first machine tool.
22. Threshing machine: Andrew Meikle invented the threshing machine in 1786.
23. Sewing machine: Thomas Saint invented the sewing machine in 1790.
24. Vaccine: Edward Jenner develops the first successful vaccine, the smallpox vaccine in 1798.
25. Paper machine: Louis-Nicolas Robert invented the first paper machine in 1799.
26. Battery: Alessandro Volta invented the earliest battery, the Voltaic pile, in 1800.
27. Morphine: Friedrich Sertürner invented Morphine in 1804.
28. Steam Locomotive: Richard Trevithick invented the steam locomotive in 1804.
29. Telegraph: Francis Ronalds invented the first telegraph in 1816.
30. Computer: Charles Babbage who was considered the 'father of the computer' built the earliest computer in 1822.

31. Electromagnet: William Sturgeon invented electromagnet in 1825.
32. Reaping machine: Patrick Bell invented the reaping machine in 1828.
33. Electric Motor: In 1934, Moritz von Jacobi invented the first electric motor.
34. Solar Cell: 1839: Edmond Becquerel invented the first solar cell in 1839.
35. Modern Portland cement: Isaac Charles Johnson invented the Modern Portland cement in 1845.
36. Rechargeable Battery: Gaston Planté invented the lead acid battery, the first rechargeable battery in 1859.
37. Steel: Carl Wilhelm Siemens and Pierre-Émile Martin invented the Siemens-Martin process for making steel in 1865.
38. Dynamite: Alfred Nobel invented Dynamite in 1867.
39. Stainless Steel: J.E.T. Woods and J. Clark invented Stainless steel in 1872.
40. Electrical Generator: Zénobe Gramme invented the first commercial electrical generator in 1873.
41. Telephone: Alexander Graham Bell has a patent granted for the telephone in 1876, who was considered to be the father of Telephone.
42. Phonograph: Thomas Edison invented the first working phonograph in 1877.
43. Electric bulb: In 1879, the patent for Incandescent light bulb was given to Joseph Swan and Thomas Edison and they were considered to be the inventor of light bulb.
44. Bicycle: John Kemp Starley invented the modern bicycle in 1885.
45. Dry Cell Battery: Carl Gassner invents the zinc-carbon battery, the first dry cell battery in 1886.

46. Car: Karl Benz invents the first petrol or gasoline powered auto-mobile (car) in 1886.
47. Ballpoint Pen: John J. Loud invented the ballpoint pen in 1888.
48. Zipper: Whitcomb Judson invented the zipper in 1891.
49. Cinematograph: Léon Bouly invented the cinematograph in 1892.
50. Diesel Engine: Rudolf Diesel invented the diesel engine in 1893.
51. X-ray: Wilhelm Conrad Röntgen invented the X-ray in 1895.
52. Air Conditioner: The first modern electrical Air Conditioner was invented by Willis Carrier in 1902.
53. Aeroplane: Aeroplane was invented by Orville and Wilbur Wright in 1903.
54. Television: Philo Farnsworth, John Logie Baird and Charles Francis Jenkins were the pioneer of the invention of Television in the early 1900s.
55. Washing machine: The first electric-powered washing machine was invented by Alva J. Fisher and introduced in 1908 by the Hurley Machine Company of Chicago, Illinois.
56. Refrigerator: Refrigerator for home and domestic use was invented by Fred W. Wolf in 1913.
57. Penicillin: Penicillin is invented by Alexander Fleming in 1928.
58. Electron microscope: The electron microscope is invented by Ernst Ruska in 1931.
59. FM Radio: Edwin H. Armstrong invented FM Radio in 1933.
60. Programmable computer: Konrad Zuse built the first freely programmable computer (Z1) in the world in 1938.

61. Polyester: Polyester is invented by British scientists John Whinfield and James Dickson in 1941.
62. Transistor: The transistor is invented by John Bardeen and Walter Brattain under the supervision of William Shockley in December 1947.
63. Video Tape recorder: The first video tape recorder is invented by Norikazu Sawazaki in 1953.
64. DNA: Watson and Crick Discovered DNA on February 28th, 1953.
65. Hard Disk Drive: The hard disk drive is invented by IBM in 1956.
66. Artificial Satellite: The first artificial satellite, Sputnik 1, is built and launched by the Soviet Union in 1957.
67. IC (integrated circuit): The integrated circuit is invented by Jack Kilby and Robert Noyce in 1958-59.
68. Pocket Calculator: The pocket calculator is invented in Japan in 1970.
69. Internet: The Internet protocol suite is developed by Vinton Cerf and Robert E. between 1973-1975.
70. Cell phone: The first commercially available cell phone, the DynaTAC 8000X, is created by Motorola in 1984. Now mobile phone (Smartphone) became the most famous using device in the world and everyday life without smartphone is unthinkable.
71. W.W.W. (World Wide Web): The World Wide Web is first introduced to the public by English engineer and computer scientist Sir Tim Berners-Lee in 1990.

(N.B: Only few are included in the list as including all the inventions would take immense space and time)

We cannot imagine life without the aforementioned inventions in our day-to-day life and no man can deny the necessity of science in our everyday life. Science has helped and eased the pain of the people in every aspect. For transportation, science built vehicles like airplane, train, cars, etc. enabling us to travel around the world in a day which would take a year by foot. To entertain us in time of our stressful moment, science have made available for us entertainment accessories like radio, TV, Smartphone and other electronics. The best example we can find is Smartphone, making the world as small as our palm and which became indispensable to the people of every ages.

To ease us from our household chore, it provided us washing machine, refrigerator, microwave, stove, garbage cleaner, dishwasher etc. Science has provided us clothes to protect us from cold and air conditioner from heat. To make our daily end meet, science have built tractor, tiller, harvester and produce fertilizer, insecticide, pesticide etc. to increases crop productivity. Science have invented medical drug to cure our different sicknesses and ailments.

Through science, human have built cities. This makes it clear that we cannot live without science. From the moment we get up to the time we go to sleep and even in our sleep, we depend on science.

Now, seeing all the successful journey of science, scientists and many others gave all the credits of inventions and discoveries to science. When all those marvelous inventions were brought to discussion, enthusiastic devotee of science claimed the supremacy of science above everything who thought that the super brain of human who study science makes it all happened.

And now questions were being asked; science has contributed so many things to the world. What we eat is come through science. What we wear is from science and wherever we go, we depend on science. And everything that we need is supplied by science and we will not be able to live without science. What has God provided or do for us? Look at the world today. Technology played a huge role in the human society. The best example is Smartphone which became one of the most useful tools in our life, using by young and old alike, regardless of rich and poor. Can we imagine a month without Smartphone by our side? What has God and his followers contribute to the world? What have missionary, the so-called messenger of God do for the world today?

Do you think their questions were appropriate to be asked, having seeing the world need science to help us survive and to comfort?

Science has been indeed a blessing; and it is true that all the things we use today is created/invented by science, however, the success of science makes many of us worship it as if science is a god without realizing the source of all the success science is making. Even though the civilization of the world as we now are has been made possible with the advancement of technology, thanks to the development of science, there is one thing that need to emphasis upon. We all know that science did not exist from the beginning of the creation of the Earth. Even before the consideration of science as a subject in the academic field which began in the Seventeenth century, many inventions and discoveries has been made.

Science alone cannot create or invent things without the wisdom of men put into it. And where did wisdom come from? According to the Origin of Species by Charles Darwin which is accepted by almost all the scientists and its subordinates, men were evolved from an ape which is cent percent animal. When I do research for the most intelligent animal in the world, I could see different answers from different blog or article.

The Ranker ranked Orangutan at No. 1, followed by Bottlenose Dolphin. Chimpanzee came at third and Elephant, Crow, African Grey Parrot, Pig, Rat, at fourth, fifth, sixth, seventh and eighth. (Please refer to original article for details: https://www.ranker.com/list/the-15-smartest-animals-on-earth/analise.dubner)

List25 ranked Orangutan at twentieth behind pigeon. Whale is included in the top5 where parrot stand at fourth, bottlenose dolphin at third and second and first position were occupied by pig and chimpanzee. (Please refer to original article for details: https://www.list25.com/25-most-intelligent-animals-on-earth/)

From Treehugger, we have the top 5 smartest animals: Raven, Dolphin, Rat, Pig and Bonobo. (Please refer to original article for details: https://www.treehugger.com/smartest-animals-earth-4864285)

BBC Earth Top 10 most intelligent animals: 10. Capuchin, 9. Kea, 8. Orangutan , 7. Caledonian Crow, 6. Ant, 5. Carrion Crow, 4. Octopus, 3. Elephant, 2. Dolphin, 1. Chimpanzee. (Please refer to original article: https://www.bbc.com/future/article/20140117-top-ten-smart-animals)

What is the conclusion? Which one of them should we recognize as the ideal one?

If an ape is defined as any tailless primate of the families such as gibbon, chimpanzee, bonobo, orangutan, gorilla, human being evolve from any of them. Man did not came from any of them.

From the beginning of the Earth, God created human

being differently; setting apart from all other living organisms. He created man with extra efforts.
When the earth was created, God only spoke the word, and it was done.
Then God said, "Let there be light"; and there was light. - Genesis 1:3 (NKJV)
"Let the waters under the heavens be gathered together into one place, and let the dry land appear"….." - Genesis 1: 9 (NKJV)
God spoke the words and the sea and dry land separated.
"Let the earth bring forth grass, the herb that yields seed, and the fruit tree that yields fruit according to its kind, whose seed is in itself, on the earth…." - Genesis 1: 11(NKJV)
God spoke the words and all kind of grasses and trees filled the land.
"Let the waters abound with an abundance of living creatures, and let birds fly above the earth across the face of the firmament of the heavens." - Genesis 1: 20(NKJV)
God spoke the words and all kind of fishes and birds came into being.
"Let the earth bring forth the living creature according to its kind: cattle and creeping thing and beast of the earth, each according to its kind..."
-Genesis 1: 24(NKJV)
God spoke the words and all kind of animals; domestic and wild, large and small, were created.
And the Lord God formed man of the dust of the ground, and breathed into his nostrils the breath of life; and man became a living being. - Genesis 2: 7(NKJV)
But when God decided to created man, God did not only

spoke but work with his own hand. He formed man by his hand unlike the other things created. God took some soil from the ground and formed out of it. Then He breathed into man's nostrils, the life giving breath and thus man began to live. Then God created woman out of man's rib so that man will love his woman and she will respect her man.

And He created man in his own image.

Then God said, "Let Us make man in Our image, according to Our likeness; let them have dominion over the fish of the sea, over the birds of the air, and over the cattle, over all the earth and over every creeping thing that creeps on the earth."

- Genesis 1: 26 (NKJV)

So God created man in His own image, in the image of God He created him; male and female He created them. - Genesis 1: 27 (NKJV)

God created man with different purpose, putting all the ingredients of wisdom fit to rule the earth, and making all other living organism inferior to man. He makes all the things on earth under the control of man.

Then God blessed them, and God said to them, "Be fruitful and multiply; fill the earth and subdue it; have dominion over the fish of the sea, over the birds of the air, and over every living thing that moves on the earth." - Genesis 1: 28 (NKJV)

God gave man, the wisdom to rule the earth; over the smallest living organism to the biggest animal that is on earth. If man was evolved from an apes, thing would have been completely different today. Science clearly told us that for one thing to evolve into another thing would take millions of years. And if their theories are to believe, human cannot be as wise as today, for the brain will have to slowly transformed from that of Homo sapiens to modern man.

And do you still not understand why the mightiest animal on earth, elephant whose weight is hundreds of hundred more than man still submitted to man? It was God's command that even the mightiest animal will submit to man.

Do you not understand lion, the mightiest animal in the forest move back at the sight of man?

If man were of ape, do you think elephant would readily submit to man who is inferior to them in size and in strength?

God gave to man, the wisdom and knowledge to rule the world. He gave the knowledge of how to invent thing for uses and how to discover thing unknown to man before that man may enjoy it after. God may not provides us in person the thing we need but gave to man the knowledge of inventing it.

And so, when God gave to a person the wisdom and idea of inventing a car, that man invented it and people enjoy the fruit of its invention. We cannot expect, and it would be too wrong as well for us to wait for God to provide us the thing we need when we open our eyes. If God were to give each of us the thing we need, what would be the success of science? And who would toil so hard to build machine?

In His wisdom, God provide the ideas and wisdom to science and in turn, science made machine for our uses. God can give wisdom to any man He desired for all the wisdom, knowledge and understanding belongs to Him, however, God did not instill all the wisdom of the world to

men so that man will not get the opportunity to place themselves equal to God. Having seen different machines were built by different man in different period of time, we cannot proclaim one person as the greatest of all men. To one person, God gave the ability to build a car, and to another, He gave the ability to build crane. He gave to one person the ability to judge, and to another, He gave the ability to sing or dance. And when all of these come together, it forms a community of interdependence, and to make the people realize that no man can live by himself.
"With Him is wisdom and strength, he hath counsel and understanding."

Job
12: 13

All things, living or non-living were in His hand. And no man can complain Him about it. It is His choice whether to make you rise or make you fall; or to make you master over somebody or make you a servant to somebody.
Therefore, a person cannot boast about his ability of doing thing which other haven't done before because it is God who is the author of his knowledge and wisdom. It would be rather more blessed to praise God for giving you the insight than to make yourself popular in the eyes of the people. God gave you the wisdom with a purpose and when you couldn't fulfill that purpose, God is not unable to take away your knowledge and understanding. He can make you a fool in no time as well.
"In whose hand is the soul of every living thing, and the breath of all mankind."

Job 12: 10

Now, what the missionary has done for the world is needed to study deeper. God did not make man to rule the world at one's own liking. He made each of us for a purpose. When we were at ourselves, the only thing that make us happy is to pleasure ourselves; be it satisfaction over the success we has accumulated or taking the pleasure of people's praise while the facilitated of God on us is placed at secondary or not remember at all. God did not like that. Just as we want people's gratitude at our help, God too wants us to appreciate those that He had helped us. Despite his unfailing love, we often choose to turn away from Him and go serve other master who cannot give us satisfaction we were seeking. And as we were often overlooking Him for all the things he had done for us, He sent his missionary to announce the necessity of turning back to Him. For God did not want a single soul to be lost.

"For what is a man profited, if he shall gain the whole world, and lose his own soul? Or what shall a man give in exchange for his soul?"

Matthew 16: 26

Chapter 9 Science And God

We can clearly see that science is not a created thing that can be experimented. It is not created or developed by a single person or by a group of people, but is developed over time and join together to study and to give knowledge about nature and thing happening around us. And with the advancement of technologies, the field of study about nature becomes broader and deeper. Science doesn't come as a fully shaped object from the beginning and is still growing. That is why it's not exactly the same now as it is when it is first developed. In short, science is the study which gives knowledge to men. And the word Scientist was first coined by William Whewell in 1833. Prior to that, scientists were called natural philosophers.

The earliest roots of science can be traced to ancient Egypt and Mesopotamia in around 3000 to 1200 BC. Science and its field has improves greatly since then with the Scientific Revolution that came from 15th centuries in Europe which transformed the view about nature and rising of machines.

The advancement of science and its technologies helps us understand what was hidden from us in the past. Many great things were invented and discovered along with human civilization. One of the first greatest inventions is the wheel, probably invented about 5500 years ago which altered the history of mankind. After the invention of the wheel, many greater things and machines were invented years after years. One of such great inventions is the printing press which was invented by Johannes Gutenberg of France in 1439, followed by the invention of Telephone by Alexander Graham Bill in 1876. Light bulb was then invented in 1879 by Thomas Alva Edison and Automobile in 1885 by Karl Friedrich Benz. There were countless of inventions that bring the world into modernization but only few inventions were listed here, for complete inclusion of inventions would take a book to fill.

Now, we enjoy the effort science has been doing all these years. Back in 1700s, there isn't any automobile and travelling is a challenging job, needing time and our effort but now, traveling is not a matter of hardship anymore. We can even travel around the world in just two days or three. Delivering news from one place to another is a time consuming job in the past. It is just a phone call away now. The world is dark prior to the invention of bulb. We can even work at night just like during daytime now. The world was often hit hard by diseases that seem not irrepressible forever, like Leprosy that comes and routed the life of human into frantic turmoil but medical science has defeated the disease and now we have nothing to panic about. The medical science has developed so much now that diseases that are life threatening in the past are not a problem anymore.

Human had even set foot on the moon which is about 384,400 km away from our Earth on June 20th 1969. There's no way we could manually measure the distance of the Earth and the moon or how big our Earth is. But science makes it possible. Now, we understand that our Earth is measured up to about 40,075 km in equatorial circumference and weighting 6.6 sextillion tons having

about 510 million square km of surface area.
Without science, we might still assume that the universe holds a lone planet Earth and the Venus we see is just another common star. Through its research, we now understand that there are other seven planets apart from our Earth in the universe and our planet is spherical in shape.
Science today is not the same as science in the 1800s or 1900s. Technology has innovated and transformed rapidly making our life much easier than we were in the 1990s. Science will keep on marveling us through its discoveries and inventions but our God is even greater than science.
Though sciences were doing a marvelous job, there were still many things that science cannot answer or prove by their experiment leaving the fact that science is not perfect. Science can only do investigation or test on things that can be seen, touch and experimented. They have no power on thing which cannot be seen or touch. Since Science can only do experiment on thing that can be seen and touch, how can science prove or disprove the existence of God who cannot be seen or touch?
For example, science does not know what is inside the black hole. Though astronomers have the knowledge of black hole, they have no clue what lies at the bottom of the black hole and it still remain a mystery.
The presence of ghost is also debating for centuries. Many have claimed to have sighted ghosts, and horror movies on ghost were also been produced. Many of us believe in the spirit of the death walking on Earth. Thousands of photos, videos, and sightings of ghosts have been accumulated, but no scientific proof has ever been found. Both ghost hunters and scientists have used electromagnetic field

detectors and thermal imaging to try and find scientific evidence of their existence but to no avail. At the end, most scientists believe these sightings are caused purely by mental phenomena, electrical fields, and ocular vibrations. Just because they cannot do experiment on ghost since it cannot be touch. The theories put up by science can neither be proven nor disproven, leaving the existence of ghosts still in question.

Science is still working on what is the universe made of. Astronomers believed that majority of the universe is made up of two things: dark matter which bind the galaxies together and dark energy that push the universe's expansion. But it is said that dark matter and dark energy are invisible to light and electromagnetic radiation making it impossible to detect or understand what they actually are. The question is still left unanswered. How vast is our universe and how many stars are actually there in the galaxy? We need not necessarily know about it but when such question is raise, science would takes time to get an answer, perhaps taking thousand more years to find it or probably left unanswered forever.

We understand that people do dream in their sleep and there should be a reason and purpose that we dreamt dreams. Oneirologist described that most dreaming were occurs during Rapid Eye movement (REM) sleep caused by brainstem activation during REM sleep and stimulate the limbic system and that all dreams doesn't mean anything which are merely electrical brain impulses that pull random thoughts and imagery from our memories. But they couldn't explain as to why we envisage strange images when we sleep. Sometime we dream about thing we haven't seen in real life at all. And how will science explain

why we sometime dream ourselves flying in the sky without any support?
Science couldn't find out how we stored memories in our brain. They have no clue why only human being can understand and have knowledge of what is good and what is bad. They have no knowledge what preceded the Big Bang. They do not understand exactly why we move forward with time and why time is always persistence and going the same direction forever. Yawning is still a mystery to science. We yawned when we feel sleepy or tired or hungry. We all know that, but also yawned when we wake up and not tired at all. And sometime we just yawn when we saw somebody near us yawning. We all know that ice is liquid. But when it was frozen, why does ice get slippery and why do warm water froze faster than the cold water? Science is still trying to find why. We may think that cats purr when they were happy and calm. But science is still unsure why cat purr because studies of feline behavior have found out that cats also purr when they are hungry, sleepy, frightened and when they are by themselves. Science doesn't understand how placebo effect works. List can go on and on.
We have seen the greatness of science. Thousands of inventions are too good for a mere compliment. We cannot imagine life without science in our day to day life. The comfort they gives, health facility they provides, technologies and machineries they assist to our life is something that is praiseworthy. Our live is much easier and pleasurable than the life in olden days. However, despite all these marvelous deed, science is still not everything to be worship. Because of the contribution they made to the human civilization makes them proud and conceited but

there is surely something behind their greatness. And that was God. God, who controlled everything.

When we talk about God, many peoples will not want to admit it. They will even demand proof of his existence experimentally. As we all know that God have no bodily shape and cannot be seen or touch to be test or experimented, it is beyond what we can envision. But that doesn't mean that there is no God just because he cannot be tested or experimented. God is spirit who is omnipotent, omnipresent and omniscient. And I can boldly claim that He is behind every creation in the universe and on earth.

In fact, God did not created machine practically and gave it to men for use. But He gave the insight to particular person(s) to create it. Just look at how man flourished. Thousands of different kind of machines makes our life beautiful, comfortable and easy. But those machines were not invented by a single person or just a group of scientist but by different person at different occasion of time.

Isaac Newton discovered the law of gravity but he depends on other persons for the thing he needed. Galileo Galilei who was also known as "the father of Modern Science" may have contributed many great things in the field of cosmos world but he probably didn't invent any machine that human can be used at. The invention of telephone by Alexander Graham Bell is noteworthy but he didn't invented automobile that made traveling much easier. Wright brothers invented the first plane but they didn't invent Internet that we enjoyed today. No person has ever invented or discovered everything. One person invented one thing and the other persons invented or discovered another thing. In this way, men depend on each other for survival and building the world together. No man had ever heard God telling a person that He would give the insight of creating a certain thing or machine but it is He who gave men the insight to invent and discover what has invented and discovered so far. In his wisdom, He allows no one to have all the knowledge in the world. He made one person mastered on one thing and to other person another thing. He gave each one of us different talent that we may help each other in order to continue living in harmony. That is why, Isaac Newton may have the greatest knowledge about gravity than anybody else but he cannot do what Galileo has done. Likewise, Vinton Cerf and Robert E. may have developed Internet before anybody does but they cannot do what Charles Babbage has done for the world.

"And he gave some, apostles; and some, prophets; and some, evangelists; and some, pastors and teachers;" Ephesians 4:11

God allow no one to have all the insight for he knew that giving everything or even half of the knowledge in the world to one person would definitely mean disaster. We have seen how many scientists have begun to claim about God when science become better and better. We have seen how inventions and discoveries make people proud and conceited, as if they did everything by themselves. A person who have invented or discovered one or two things makes them snobbish. How much more would he become if God gave hundred abilities?

Have you ever imagined why out of million species of animals, only human being has understanding and knowledge? Some animals like dog or dolphin can understand some of the thing we said or order them to do it if we train them well but they cannot think for themselves. Apes weren't that much intelligent, not even reaching 10 % of what human being can understand. So, if human beings were evolved from the apes, why are we having so much intelligent and understanding?

And why do huge and powerful animals afraid of us? We have seen the biggest land animal like elephant doesn't protest and go free when they were tie on their feet by a tiny rope. They won't want to be tied up and could easily break free but they didn't. Camel and donkey will never want to carry heavy load on their back but they just obey when men wants them to carry. Horse will never want to carry men on their back and go for war but they just obey when their master order them. Lion or tiger can easily devour us but they just go at the sight of us. Why is the world favouring us?

We should understand that we are not the descendant of the ape as evolutionists have it said. No matter how much scientist claimed this way, I will never accept an ape as my ancestor in my life. If we were evolved from an ape, we will not have this much insight, intelligent or knowledge. God made human being completely different from other animals from the very beginning. After creating all that the earth should hold, He created man to nurture and look after what He had created. No man will ever want to create something and hide it. Likewise, God did not want his creation to keep it for himself so He created man to appreciate what He had created and be thankful at, for no animal has the ability to understand and appreciate their creator.

The Old Testament, first book of the Christian's Holy Bible was written at different times between about 1200

and 165 BC before the modern science flourished. There are some facts that the Holy Bible had mentioned before the science do and afterwards science prove it accurate. In the book of Isaiah 40: 22 says that the Earth is round.
"It is He who sits above the circle of the earth, And its inhabitants are like grasshoppers, Who stretches out the heavens like curtain, And spreads them out like a tent to dwell in." (NKJV)
Aristotle declared that the earth is spherical through his observation but it was Eratosthenes who had estimated the Earth's circumference to be about 46,250 Kilometers in around 240 BC.
The book of Job declared that our earth is hanged on nothing.
He stretches out the north over empty space; He hangs the earth on nothing.
-Job 26:7 (NKJV)
Now science also holds that our Earth is hanged on nothing.
In Leviticus 17:11 stated that the blood is the source of life.
"For the life of the flesh is in the blood, and I have given it to you upon the alter to make atonement for your souls; for it is the blood that makes atonement for the soul."
And in Genesis 9:4 said, "But you shall not eat flesh with its life, that is, its blood."
Later in 1618, William Harvey, an English physician discovered that blood circulated around the body by the heart through arteries and then blood return back to the heart through the veins. Then after 283 years later, Blood groups (ABO) were discovered by Karl Landsteiner in 1901 and other blood groups were also gradually

discovered after that. Now, we all know that we will die if our heart stops pumping blood into our body.

God, supernatural being, does not live among men physically but was always there among us. And He wants the best out of us. He doesn't merely created man to let them enjoy what He had created but to nurture and also to appreciate it.

Human civilization had witness different plagues and epidemics raged the world in many occasion in the history of mankind. Those plagues and epidemics and diseases doesn't come by chance but perhaps with a purpose from God. God might send different diseases at different occasions in the history of human civilization that science will keeps working to find an answer when one thing is countered successfully. He wants to show that when He is angry, science have no power to overturn it. Look at leprosy that kills millions of people but medical science takes many years to find cure. Malaria is first found in 1880s but until 1992, about more than 100 years of its first detection, find cure. It has been found out that HIV AIDS is first spread in 1920s with no human knowledge about its disease up until 1980s when French virologist Luc Antoine Montagnier and American physician-scientist Robert Charles Gallo discovered AIDS virus and no vaccine for HIV and AIDS have been discover so far. Cancer has been with us for thousands of years now but medical science is still trying hard to get the cure. This shows that science still has lot of things to do.

Science changes almost every day and will become even greater and better each day but God never changed and always will be. Even when science has finished discovered that is left to be discovered in the universe, God will still be there.

Chapter 10 End Of The World

The question about the end of the world entices many people from science to religious personality to make their own predictions.

As we are threaten by nuclear war with more and more countries possess nuclear weapons, many of us assumed that nuclear war would wipe out the human race from the face of the earth.

As declared by the NASA, the earth's surface temperature increase is said to have nearly doubled in the last 50 years, and the global warming became one of the biggest environmental issues resulting to the fear of the earth becoming too hot for human survival.

Just as the extinction of dinosaur is caused by comet, asteroid or meteor as many scientist suggested, many believes then that it would also cause the extinction of human race from the earth. Based upon their theories, calculations and beliefs, many came up with their predictions on when the earth would end.

Below are the estimated dates by various scientists or groups of scientists on which the earth will come to an end: (The below lists are extracted from the Wikipedia)

1. Nick Bostrom predicted that 500,000 years from now, Earth will have likely been hit by an asteroid of roughly 1 km in diameter during this period, assuming it cannot be averted. Bostrom writes "In order to cause the extinction

of human life, the impacting body would probably have to be greater than 1 km in diameter (and probably 3 - 10 km)".

2. The Geological Society has estimated that 1 million years from now, the Earth will likely have undergone a supervolcanic eruption large enough to erupt 3,200 km of magma, an event comparable to the Toba supereruption 75,000 years ago.

3. Stephen A. Nelson predicted that 100 million year from now, the Earth will have likely been hit by an asteroid about 10–15 km in diameter (comparable in size to the one that triggered the K–Pg extinction which killed dinosaurs 66 million years ago), assuming it cannot be averted.

4. James Kasting had calculated that after 500 million year from now, the level of carbon dioxide in the atmosphere will drop dramatically, making Earth uninhabitable.

5. 500–600 millionAnne Minard has estimated that 500 to 600 million years from now, a gamma ray burst, or massive, hyperenergetic supernova, will occurs within 6,500 light-years of Earth which is close enough for its rays to affect Earth's ozone layer and potentially trigger a mass extinction, assuming the hypothesis is correct that a previous such explosion triggered the Ordovician–Silurian extinction event.

6. Many scientists had estimated that 1 to 5 billion years from now, the Sun's current phase of development would end, after which it will swell into a red giant, either swallowing Earth or at least completely scorching it.

7. S. Franck, C. Bounama and W. Von BlohIt's estimated that all the Eukaryotic life will die out due to carbon dioxide starvation and only prokaryotes will remain after 1.3 billion years from now.

7. David Powell had claimed to have estimated that the Earth and the Moon will be most likely destroyed by falling into the Sun after 7.59 billion years from now, just before the Sun reaches the tip of its red giant phase and its maximum radius of 256 times the present day value.
8. Various scientists had estimated that 10 billion years from now, the heat death of the universe is a scientific theory in which the universe will diminish to a state of no thermodynamic free energy and therefore will no longer sustain motion or life.
Not only secular scientists had predicted the end of the earth but also many others from different religious groups and even some Christians (false Christian, I should say) predicted based on the eschatological events described on their sacred scriptures. We will look at their predictions below:
Past dates
1. 66–70 AD: Simon bar Giora, Jewish Essenes: The Essene sect of Jewish ascetics saw the Jewish revolt against the Romans in 66–70 in Judea as the final end-time battle which would bring about the arrival of the Messiah. By the authority of Simon, coins were minted declaring the redemption of Israel. It did not happened.
2. 365 AD: Hilary of Poitiers: The early French bishop announced the end of the world would happen during this year. It did not happened.
3. 375–400AD: Martin of Tours: The French bishop stated that the world would end before 400 AD, writing, "There is no doubt that the Antichrist has already been born, firmly established already in his early years, he will, after reaching maturity, achieve supreme power." It did not happened.

4. 500 AD: Hippolytus of Rome, Sextus Julius Africanus and Irenaeus: All three of them predicted Jesus would return in this year with one of the predictions being based on the dimensions of Noah's ark. It did not happened.
5. April 6, 793 AD: Beatus of Liébana: The Spanish monk prophesied the second coming of Christ and the end of the world on that day in front of a large crowd of people. It did not happened.
6. 800AD: Sextus Julius Africanus: He revised the date of Doomsday to the year 800. It did not happened.
7. 799–806AD: Gregory of Tours: The French bishop calculated the End would occur between the years 799 and 806. It did not happened.
8. 848AD: Thiota: Thiota declared that the world would end during this year. It did not happened.
9. 992–995AD: Various Christians: Good Friday coincided with the Feast of the Annunciation; this had long been believed to be the event that would bring forth the Antichrist, and thus the end-times, within 3 years. It did not happened.
10. January 1, 1000 AD: Various Christian clerics including Pope Sylvester II predicted the end of the world on this date. Riots occurred in Europe and pilgrims headed east to Jerusalem. It did not happened.
11. 1033AD: Various Christians: Following the failure of the January 1, 1000 prediction, some theorists proposed that the end would occur 1000 years after Jesus' death, instead of his birth. It did not happened.
12. Late 1000s AD: Various Christians: Leading up to the Crusades, many people made pilgrimage to Jerusalem in hope of being saved, for the "dread day of wrath was upon them: men no longer tilled the earth, fearing the end of all

things". It did not happened.

13. 1260AD: Joachim of Fiore: The Italian mystic determined that the Millennium would begin between 1200 and 1260. It did not happened.

14. 1284AD: Pope Innocent III: The Pope predicted that the world would end 666 years after the rise of Islam. It did not happened.

15: 1290 and 1335AD: The followers of Joachim of Fiore rescheduled the end of the world to 1290 and then again to 1335 when his 1260 prophecy failed. It failed again.

16. 1346–1351AD: Various Europeans: The black plague spreading across Europe was interpreted by many as the sign of the end of times. It did not happened.

17. 1370AD: Jean de Roquetaillade: The Antichrist was to come in 1366 and the Millennium would begin either in 1368 or 1370. It did not happened.

18. 1378AD: Arnaldus de Villa Nova: This Joachite wrote that the Antichrist was to come during this year. It did not happened.

19. 1504AD: Sandro Botticelli believed he was living during the Tribulation, and that the Millennium would begin in three and a half years from 1500. He wrote into his painting The Mystical Nativity that the Devil was loose and would soon be chained. It did not happened.

20. February 1, 1524AD: London astrologers: A group of astrologers in London predicted the world would end by a flood starting in London, based on calculations made the previous June. 20,000 Londoners left their homes and headed for higher ground in anticipation. It did not happened.

21. 1656AD: Christopher Columbus: In his 'Book of Prophecies (1501)', Columbus predicted that the world

would end during this year. It did not happened.
22. 1657AD: Fifth Monarchists: This group of radical Christians predicted that the final apocalyptic battle and the destruction of the Antichrist were to take place between 1655 and 1657. It did not happened.
23. 1658AD: Christopher Columbus: He claimed that the world was created in 5343 BC, and would last 7000 years. Assuming no year zero, that means the end would come in 1658. It did not happened.
24. 1660AD: Joseph Mede: Mede claimed that the Antichrist had appeared in 456, and the end would come in 1660. It did not happened.
25. 1666AD: Sabbatai Zevi: Following his failed prediction of 1648, Zevi recalculated the end of the Earth for this year. It failed again.
26. 1666AD: Fifth Monarchists: The presence of 666 in the date, the death of 100,000 Londoners to bubonic plague, and the Great Fire of London led to superstitious fears of the end of the world from some Christians. It did not happened.
27. 1673AD: William Aspinwall: This Fifth Monarchist claimed the Millennium would begin by this year. It did not happened.
28. 1688AD: John Napier: This mathematician calculated the end of the world would be this year based on calculations from the Book of Revelation. It did not happened.
29. 1689AD: Pierre Jurieu: This prophet predicted that Judgment Day would occur this year.
It did not happened.
30. 1694AD: John Mason and Johann Heinrich: This two predicted the Millennium would begin by this year. Johann

Jacob also believed that Jesus would return and the world would end this year. It did not happened.

31. 1697AD: Cotton Mather: This Puritan minister predicted the world would end this year. After the prediction failed, he revised the date of the End two more times. It did not happened.

32. 1700AD: John Napier: After his 1688 prediction failed to come true, Napier revised his end of the world prediction to this year. It failed again.

33. 1700–1734AD: Nicholas of Cusa: This Cardinal predicted the end would occur between 1700 and 1734. It did not happened.

34. 1736AD: Cotton Mather: Mather's third and final prediction for the end of the world.

It never happened.

35. 1757AD: Emanuel Swedenborg: Swedenborg claimed that the Last Judgment occurred in the spiritual world this year. It did not happened.

36. May 19, 1780AD: Connecticut General Assembly members, New Englanders: The sky turning dark during the day was interpreted as a sign of the end times. The primary cause of the event is believed to have been a combination of smoke from forest fires, a thick fog, and cloud cover. It did not happened.

37. 1789AD: Pierre d'Ailly: The year 1789 would bring the coming of the Antichrist, according to this 14th-century Cardinal. It did not happened.

38. 1794AD: Shakers: He predicted the world would end in both the years 1792 and 1794.

It did not happened.

39. November 19, 1795AD: Nathaniel Brassey Halhed: While campaigning for Richard Brothers' release, Halhead

proclaimed that the world would end on this day. It did not happened.

40. 1793–1795AD: Richard Brothers: This retired sailor stated the Millennium would begin between the years 1793 and 1795. He was eventually committed to an insane asylum.

It did not happened.

41. 1805AD: Christopher Love: This Presbyterian minister predicted the destruction of the world by earthquake in 1805, followed by an age of everlasting peace when God would be known by all. It did not happened.

42. 1836AD: Johann Albrecht Bengel: In the 1730s he proclaimed that, based on a careful study of the prophecies of the Bible, Judgment Day would come in 1836, with the Pope as the anti-Christ and the Freemasons representing the "false prophet" of Revelations. It did not happened.

43. 1836AD: John Wesley: Wesley, the founder of the Methodist Church, foresaw the Millennium beginning this year. He wrote that Revelation 12:14 referred to the years 1058–1836, "when Christ should come". It did not happened.

44. December 31, 1843AD: Millerites: Although it was not officially endorsed by their leadership, many Millerites expected the Second Coming to occur on April 28 or at the end of 1843. It did not happened.

45. 1843AD: Harriet Livermore: The first of two years this preacher predicted the world would end. It did not happened.

46. March 21, 1844AD: William Miller: Miller predicted Christ would return on this day.

It did not happened.

47. October 22, 1844AD: Millerites: After Christ did not

return on March 21, 1844, the Millerites then revised William Miller's prediction to October 22, 1844, claiming to have miscalculated the Scripture. It did not happened.
48. August 7, 1847AD: George Rapp: Rapp, the founder of the Harmony Society, preached that Jesus would return in his lifetime, even as he lay dying on August 7, 1847.
It did not happened.
49. 1847AD: Harriet Livermore: The second prediction of the end of the world from this preacher. It did never happened.
50. 2020 AD: Jeane Dixon: Dixon claimed that Armageddon would take place in 2020, and Jesus will return to defeat the unholy trinity of the Antichrist, Satan, and the False prophet between 2020 and 2037. She had also previously predicted the world would end on February 4, 1962.
The year 2020 has passed but nothing happened.
51. 2021AD: F. Kenton Beshore: Beshore bases his prediction on the prior suggestion that Jesus would return in 1988, i.e., within one Biblical generation (40 years) of the founding of Israel in 1948. Beshore argues that the prediction was correct, but that the definition of a Biblical generation was incorrect and was actually 70–80 years, placing the Second Coming of Jesus between 2018 and 2028 and the Rapture by 2021 at the latest.
2021?
The below are more predictions made by different peoples which the date is yet to come:
1. 2026AD: Messiah Foundation International: The members predict that the world will end in 2026, when an asteroid would collide with Earth in accordance with Riaz Ahmed Gohar Shahi's predictions in The Religion of God.

The chances of asteroid hitting the Earth is said to be only 1 out of 300,000.

2. 2060AD: Isaac Newton: According to Isaac Newton's research of the Bible, Jesus will rapture his Church one jubilee from the time of Israel re-acquiring Jerusalem.

3. 2129AD: Said Nursî: According to abjad interpretation of a hadith, this Sunni Muslim theologian who wrote the Risale-i Nur Collection, which expects the end in 2129.

4. 2200AD: Various: Using a cricket analogy of the doomsday argument, the last human will be born before the start of the year 2200.

5. 2280AD: Rashad Khalifa: According to Rashad Khalifa's research on the Quran Code, the world will end during that year.

6. 11120AD: John A. Leslie: According to Leslie's figures for the doomsday argument, the last humans will be born within the next 9120 years.

Many predictions were being made which were not included in the list. A man named Jeff Williams even claimed to be a time traveler who have been traversed into the year 2061 and returned to the year 2018 to warn the Earth of comet called Halley's Comet hitting the Earth in 2061 which would result to the end of the world.

The news of such prediction when circulates around the globe, threw frenzy upheaval among (many) people who were been misled into thinking that the world would come to an end for real. Some people had even sold their properties and distributed the money to the people to at least show some humanity before they die. It's a good thing to show humanity. It's always good to help the needy. But can their last good deed without repentance save their soul?

Do not be afraid when such news comes. No such predictions will ever come true. The world will not end by war. Human race will not extinct due to asteroid or comet hitting the earth. This world will never be too hot to live on. The end of the world will not come from any of these. It will end only in one way. The Second Coming of Jesus Christ, but no one knows when.

When some Christians predicted about the end of the world, we should not be surprise at it. But how unfortunate they were! They never realized that they had made a big mistake by predicting when the world will end. Their prediction is purely based upon their own personal beliefs and interest. I am certain that many of them make their prediction so as to make themselves a prophet in the eyes of common people. Some even goes too far by falsely comparing their prediction with the quotation from the scripture. If they have thorough knowledge about the Bible, they would never make such predictions. From time to time, we heard about an asteroid passing near us, and we even heard about the possibility of hitting of the earth by an asteroid which could erase human race from the face of the earth. But worried not for the end of the world will see by not such thing. Before the end of the world come, the gospel of the kingdom of God must be preached to all corner of the earth.

Since the Bible is true, none of their predictions came true and their predictions of the future dates will never come true either. We should not worry on such thing but rather be prepared for the second coming of Jesus Christ. For when He come, He will bring along with Him; Reward of life, for His faithful followers and also condemnation to hell for the unbelievers. The choice is upon us; whether to choose life or hell.

Bible did mentioned about the persecution, of antichrist, of false prophet and the awful horror. Jesus Christ told his disciples that a time will come when false prophet will appeared. We were told that they will perform great miracles and wonders in order to deceive even God's chosen people.

Jesus plainly told us that such thing will come first.

When His disciples asked him about the time of His coming when they are on Mount Olives, Jesus answered them:

And Jesus answered and said unto them, "Take heed that no man deceive you. For many will come in My name, saying, I am the Christ; and shall deceive many. And you shall hear of wars and rumours of wars. See that you are not trouble; for all these things must come to pass, but the end is not yet. For nation will rise against nation, and kingdom against kingdom: and there will be famines, pestilences, and earthquakes in various places. All these are the beginning of sorrows. Then they will deliver you up to tribulation and kill you, and you will be hated by all nations for My name's sake. And then many will be offended, will betray one another, and will hate one another. Then many false prophets will rise up and deceive many. And because lawlessness will abound, the love of many will grow cold. But he who endures to the end shall be saved. And this gospel of the kingdom will be preached in all the world as a witness to all nations, and then the end will come."

Matthew 24: 4-14 (NKJV)

However, nowhere in the Bible did mentioned about the time and hour of the end of the world. The scripture, rather said that no one knows about the day and hour. Not

the angels in heaven and not even Jesus Christ himself. Only the father; God knows about it.
Heaven and earth will pass away, but My words will by no means pass away. But of that day and hour no one knows, not even the angels in heaven, nor the Son, but only the Father.

Mark 13: 32 (NKJV)
Jesus Christ plainly said that he didn't even know about it. So what a mere human knows about it?

Chapter 11 What Happen After Death

Science offered a direct answer; NOTHING. Soon after death, the immune system stops working and microbes spread throughout the body freely. It takes just 40 hours for bacteria to spread throughout the death body once it was buried. They feed on the body and it decomposed. And the remains are bones and hairs. There's nothing left and there's no soul or spirit to be born again.

Science asserted that once the brain stops functioning at brain death, consciousness fails to survive and ceases to exist. No life can be form after human brain is dead and scientists and philosophers were skeptic when it comes to belief in life after death.

So, what happen when a person is dead? Is death really the end of everything? Almost all religions believe in the afterlife which referred to as life after death in which an individual's consciousness continues to exist after the death of the body.

Most of the religions views on the continuation of life after death which is often take place in a spiritual realm. And in other views, the individual may be reborn into this world taking another form and begin the life cycle over again with no memory of what they have done in the previous life.

According to Hinduism, death is not the end of an individual's life as a person is born, live and die multiple times until the soul become perfected and unite with its source. In their views, the worldly body is the prison for the soul that prevents them from progressing toward freedom. Thus, when a person is dead, they cremate the dead body so that the departing soul may move toward mukti with no residual of evils entombed in the soul. But they typically do not cremate the babies, children and saints who are believed to be pure and their soul are unattached to the bodies. To escape dreaded rebirth they try to do good while they were living. In order to escape dreaded rebirth they have to achieve final emancipation (Moska). Therefore, when a devout Hindu sense death, they chanted the monosyllable 'Om' repeatedly as they believe that if it is the last word on a person's lips, it guarantee a direct passage to moska.

According to Islam, death is the termination of worldly life and the beginning of afterlife. To their belief, Allah has made this worldly life as a test and a preparation ground for the afterlife. Thus, every person has only one chance to prepare themselves for the life to come where Allah will resurrect and judge every individual and will entitle them to rewards or punishments based on their good or bad deeds.

Buddhism doesn't acknowledged supreme god but believed in life after death. They believe that death simply leads to rebirth in the form of reincarnation to new body and new life.

In fact, no experiment has ever done on the life after death and there's no scientifically proof that life is possible after death. But all the religions in the world believed in the idea of afterlife. Christianity maintained their belief in the life after physical death in the most significant approach than all the other counterparts. The principle of Christian's faith emphases on the two elements in us; physical form and soul, (though science declared that there's no soul in human body) and proclaimed the existence of Heaven and Hell where our soul will either go to heaven or hell for eternity based on our faith. Our physical life on earth is the passage to either heaven or hell. But what the Christian's faith preserve is something no other religions has epitomized. In Hinduism, living a poise life can guaranteed you a better life in your next rebirth. And Islam taught that you will be rewarded if you have done a good deed in your lifetime. To them, all your deeds, whether good or bad will be weighted and if your good deeds outnumbered the bad deeds, you will be rewarded. And the more your good deeds are, the better the reward is.

But according to Christianity, your good deed alone cannot earn you the key to heaven. No matter how many good deeds you've done in your entire life, you will still need one thing to achieve eternal life; SALVATION. And how to obtain salvation? BELIEVE.

If there is no life after death or no salvation provided by God, all the teaching of Christianity is nothing but a futile. And worshipping God would mean nothing at all. Trying to do good deeds during our life is worthless and suffered in the name of truth is pointless. What is worth trying to refrain from doing bad thing if there is no salvation? If life offers a single lifetime after which no form of life ever existed, why not we enjoy the best life we can while we are living in this world? If there is no salvation, there's no need to be categorize between sin and righteousness because in the end, there will be nothing. Both sinner and righteous person will get the same fate, DEATH. If there is no salvation, it is better to live a wicked life with luxury than suffer in the goodness sake with little to eat, because this maximum 120 years is all a person can relish and be forgotten after his death. Men made laws, labeled sin and righteousness, distinguished good and bad, convict a person criminal and declared the other innocent and lived under one law because there is afterlife or salvation.

God, the Almighty offers salvation to all mankind, but not in the form of doing good deed. For if a person can obtain salvation through good deed, there's no point of obeying his law and worshipping Him as God.

Gospel John 3: 16 says, "For God so loved the world, that He gave His only begotten Son, that whosoever believeth in Him should not perish, but have everlasting life."

Despite the world full of wickedness and evil, God still loves the people and call unto them to come back to Him. In order to save the world, God sent His only begotten Son, that through Him the world might be saved. Through His Son, God gifted the Salvation to men. And that whosoever believes in His Son and in Him shall be saved.

For by grace you have been saved through faith, and that not of yourselves; it is the gift of God, not of works, lest anyone should boast.

Ephesians 2: 8-9 (NKJV)

God sending His only begotten Son to save the world has no point at all if men can be saved or obtain salvation through good work, because any man can obtain eternal life by doing good deeds without having to believe in Jesus Christ and in God.

If salvation is based on good deed alone, an individual's deeds will be judged and weighted, and reward or punishment will come out based on it. The person will be condemned to punishment if their bad deeds exceeded the good deeds or rewarded if their good deeds exceeded the bad deeds. An atheist or anybody can obtain mercy and salvation through their good deeds. If that is the case, believing in God has no meaning at all. By doing good will not make you perfect. It is an act of showing that you are willing to obey.

A rich young man came to Jesus to get His favour by claiming that he obeyed and kept all the laws and commandments of God but was fall short when Jesus told him about what the way to eternal life truly is.

And Jesus said to him, "If you want to be perfect, go, sell what you have and give to the poor, and you will have treasure in heaven; and come, follow Me."

Matthew 19: 21-22 (NKJV)

The young man, though has kept himself from doing anything evil, couldn't obtain salvation by his good deeds when he couldn't believe in Jesus Christ and follow Him.

Jesus Christ came into this world and died for all people on the cross so that all the people might be saved through His blood. But His death and resurrection is meant for only those who believed in Him. Otherwise, anybody can obtain salvation without believing in Him by doing good deeds and what Christian preached about the Son of God, letting being persecuted by the world for His namesake would mean nothing. Believing in Him doesn't simply mean saying 'I Believe in Jesus Christ' but believe in Him completely and also do His will.

What will happen to the people who don't believe in Jesus Christ after death? God had prepared a place called Hell for people who don't believe in His Son and in Him.

Failing to believe in God and His Son will see yourself thrown into hell for eternity, for your good deed alone cannot save you. Sometime, I wondered the Christian included myself are one of the most foolish people on Earth. They were often taught and preached in the church and other fellowships of how dreadful hell is but continue to sin.

Believe in Jesus Christ and do what He command you to do, then you will be saved and have eternal life where no sorrow and pain will ever be seen.

Conclusion

Science is changing and progressing in every field every day. What is hidden today will come to light tomorrow. What is not possible today will be made possible tomorrow. What is unreachable today will be reached to tomorrow. What is unsolvable will be solved tomorrow. But science will never find a day that everything that is in the universe has been discovered or what is inventible has been invented. One thing will be discovered or invented today but there will still be thing to be invented or discovered tomorrow and science will keep on chasing that dream.

We all know that science can only do experiment on things that can touch or seen. So, when science cannot do what is beyond their reach, why are we still trying to believe in science? Haven't we already known that science is not perfect? Haven't we already known that science is only the creation of man? Haven't we already known that science is created to study the nature?

Science cannot proof the existence of God by their experiment. So, would that makes us think that there is no God because He cannot be tested scientifically? God is beyond the reach of science. But that doesn't mean that there is no God. What is not perfect (science) cannot examined on what is perfect (God). God only said to believe in Him so that we may be saved.

He said to him, "Thomas, because you have seen Me, you have believed. Blessed are those who have not seen and yet have believed." - John 20:29 (NKJV)

Through blood we lived and through blood, we are been saved. Christ has died for the sin of the world, and blessed are those who believed in Him and in God.

God bless all of you who read this book and believe in God and His Son Christ Jesus as their personal Saviour!

www.ingramcontent.com/pod-product-compliance
Lightning Source LLC
LaVergne TN
LVHW050410160726
843469LV00041B/1014

* 9 7 8 9 3 5 6 1 0 8 6 2 2 *